Lecture Notes of the Institute
for Computer Sciences, Social Informatics
and Telecommunications Engineering   668

The LNICST series publishes ICST's conferences, symposia and workshops.
LNICST reports state-of-the-art results in areas related to the scope of the Institute.
The type of material published includes

- Proceedings (published in time for the respective event)
- Other edited monographs (such as project reports or invited volumes)

LNICST topics span the following areas:

- General Computer Science
- E-Economy
- E-Medicine
- Knowledge Management
- Multimedia
- Operations, Management and Policy
- Social Informatics
- Systems

Phan Cong Vinh · Hafiz Mahfooz Ul Haque ·
Nguyen Van Han

Editors

Nature of Computation and Communication

10th EAI International Conference, ICTCC 2024
Dalat City, Vietnam, October 15–16, 2024
Proceedings

 Springer

Editors
Phan Cong Vinh
Nguyen Tat Thanh University
Ho Chi Minh City, Vietnam

Hafiz Mahfooz Ul Haque
University of Central Punjab
Johar Town, Pakistan

Nguyen Van Han
Thuy Loi University
Hanoi, Vietnam

ISSN 1867-8211   ISSN 1867-822X (electronic)
Lecture Notes of the Institute for Computer Sciences, Social Informatics
and Telecommunications Engineering
ISBN 978-3-032-12845-4   ISBN 978-3-032-12846-1 (eBook)
https://doi.org/10.1007/978-3-032-12846-1

Preface

EAI ICTCC 2024 (10th EAI International Conference on Nature of Computation and Communication), an international scientific event for research in the field of smart computing and communication, was held during October 15–16, 2024 in cyberspace, due to two reasons as follows: first, convenience for remote authors; second, the travel restrictions caused by the potential impact of the worldwide COVID-19 pandemic. The aim of the conference is to provide an internationally respected forum for scientific research in the technologies and applications of smart computing and communication. This conference provides an excellent opportunity for researchers to discuss modern approaches and techniques for smart computing systems and their applications.

The proceedings of EAI ICTCC 2024 are published by Springer in the series Lecture Notes of the Institute for Computer Sciences, Social Informatics and Telecommunications Engineering (LNICST), indexed by DBLP, EI, Google Scholar, Scopus, and Thomson ISI. For this tenth edition of EAI ICTCC, repeating the success of the previous year, the Program Committee received submissions from 8 countries and each paper was reviewed by at least three expert reviewers in a double-blind process. From 20 submissions we chose 7 papers after intensive discussions held among the Program Committee members. We truly appreciate the excellent reviews and lively discussions of the Program Committee members and external reviewers in the review process.

This year, we had two prominent invited speakers, Marie Duží from the University of Ostrava in the Czech Republic and Nguyen Anh Linh from the University of Warsaw in Poland. EAI ICTCC 2024 was jointly organized by the European Alliance for Innovation (EAI) and Nguyen Tat Thanh University (NTTU). This conference could not have been organized without the strong support of the staff members of the two organizations. We would especially like to thank Imrich Chlamtac (University of Trento) and Ivana Bujdakova (EAI) for their great help in organizing the conference.

Phan Cong Vinh
Hafiz Mahfooz Ul Haque
Nguyen Van Han

Organization

Organizing Committee

General Chair

Phan Cong Vinh — Nguyen Tat Thanh University, Vietnam

Program Chairs

Nguyen Thanh Tung — Vietnam National University, Hanoi City, Vietnam
Hafiz Mahfooz Ul Haque — University of Central Punjab, Pakistan

Sponsorship and Exhibit Chair

Vu Tuan Anh — Industrial University of Ho Chi Minh City, Vietnam

Local Chair

Bach Long Giang — Nguyen Tat Thanh University, Vietnam

Workshops Chair

Abdur Rakib — Coventry University, UK

Publicity and Social Media Chair

Pham Van Dang — Nguyen Tat Thanh University, Vietnam

Publications Chair

Phan Cong Vinh — Nguyen Tat Thanh University, Vietnam

Web Chair

Nguyen Van Han — Nguyen Tat Thanh University, Vietnam

Technical Program Committee

Anh Dinh	University of Saskatchewan, Canada
Bui Cong Giao	Saigon University, Vietnam
Chien-Chih Yu	National Cheng Chi University, Taiwan
Giacomo Cabri	University of Modena and Reggio Emilia, Italy
Hafiz Mahfooz Ul Haque	University of Central Punjab, Pakistan
Hiroshi Fujita	Gifu University, Japan
Huynh Xuan Hiep	Can Tho University, Vietnam
Hyungchul Yoon	Chungbuk National University, South Korea
Issam Damaj	Beirut Arab University, Lebanon
Manish Khare	Dhirubhai Ambani Institute of Information and Communication Technology, India
Muhammad Athar Javed Sethi	University of Engineering and Technology Peshawar, Pakistan
Ngo Ha Quang Thinh	Ho Chi Minh City University of Technology, Vietnam
Nguyen Ha Huy Cuong	Da Nang University, Vietnam
Nguyen Manh Duc	University of Ulsan, South Korea
Nguyen Thanh Hai	Can Tho University, Vietnam
Om Prakash	Hemvati Nandan Bahuguna Garhwal University, India
Pham Quoc Cuong	Ho Chi Minh City University of Technology, Vietnam
Tran Huu Tam	University of Kassel, Germany
Truong Cong Doan	International School, VNU, Vietnam
Waralak V. Siricharoen	Silpakorn University, Thailand

Contents

Improving Vegetable Disease Diagnosis with EfficientNet Versions

Anh Kim Su[(✉)], Huy Trinh Nguyen, and Hai Thanh Nguyen

Can Tho University, Can Tho, Vietnam
{sukimanh,nthai.cit}@ctu.edu.vn, huyb2105612@student.ctu.edu.vn

Abstract. Vegetables play an important role in people's daily diet. However, vegetables often have many diseases that can affect consumers' health. This study leverages the power of deep convolutional neural networks, specifically EfficientNet, in disease detection. Our study shows that EfficientNet has the potential to outperform previous studies with VGG19 and ResNet50 for diseases such as bacterial spot rot, black rot, and downy mildew. These promising results strengthen confidence in the progress of smart agriculture and its potential to improve disease detection in vegetables.

Keywords: vegetable disease · diagnosis model · deep learning

1 Introduction

Along with rapid population growth, the food supply problem for humanity is also increasing. Many countries are facing food crises, and the problem of food shortages is not new; it is still a complex problem for the whole world. One of the essential food sources that can partially solve this problem is vegetables. Their faster growth rate than other food sources can help produce a higher quantity in a shorter period.

Vegetables are an essential source of human nutrition and are believed to have health-improving benefits. Vegetables contain many antioxidants, some of which can protect against chronic diseases such as cardiovascular and cerebrovascular diseases, eye and neurological diseases, stroke, cancer, diabetes, hypertension, and blood-related diseases [1]. However, there is a big problem: vegetables are very susceptible to disease and spoilage during the growing process. That is the main issue that needs to be resolved to minimize the current food shortage situation. Farmers used their experience to identify diseases on vegetables in the past, but this could be due to subjective issues or a lack of experience, causing the disease to be misdiagnosed, leading to not being able to cure the existing disease and costing money. So, there needs to be a solution to diagnose diseases in vegetables more accurately and quickly on a large scale. With the development of technology, plant disease diagnosis techniques based on deep learning and computer vision models have been researched and developed to solve the above

P. Cong Vinh et al. (Eds.): ICTCC 2024, LNICST 668, pp. 1–14, 2026.
https://doi.org/10.1007/978-3-032-12846-1_1

problem; data sources are also being developed and made publicly available to give developers more data for training.

In this research topic, we will limit the scope to a specific type of vegetable, cauliflower, because it is a popular vegetable grown worldwide to ensure the uniformity of input data. Ensure the model can learn the exact type of disease. In addition, cauliflower is a nutritious vegetable because it contains a lot of fat, protein, vitamins, and other nutrients [2]. Cauliflower is also recommended to prevent cancer, but it has high requirements for cultivation compared to other vegetables of the same type [3]. In this paper, we propose a deep learning model using the transfer learning method with the EfficientNet network to detect some diseases early.

The paper is structured as follows: Sect. 2 presents related research, the methods used, and their effectiveness. Section 3 introduces the dataset, the applied preprocessing and data augmentation methods, and the proposed model. Section 4 discusses the evaluation indicators used and the proposed model's results. In Sect. 5, conclusions are drawn, and future prospects are discussed.

2   Related Work

To meet the increasing demand for quality and quantity, using more technology and computer vision techniques is an option to help reduce costs and increase speed. If the disease has time to develop, it can spread to many other plants, causing massive harvest loss. For this reason, many models are built to continuously observe and detect diseases that vegetable plants suffer from as soon as possible, helping to minimize the impact on quality and quantity. The DFYOLOv5m-M2 transformer model proposed by Sun et al. [4] uses a technique called dense image annotation to be able to diagnose diseases the same way experts diagnose diseases, increasing user confidence in the model; this method provides a relatively high accuracy of 94.7%. Pradhan et al. [5] belong to Vellore Institute of Technology University, used four types of models to classify cauliflower diseases, including EfficientNetB3, DenseNet121, VGG19 CNN, and ResNet50. The result is that model-based EfficientNetB3 has the highest accuracy rate with 98% and other models, respectively VGG19 CNN with 84%, DenseNet121 with 81%, and the lowest is ResNet50 with 78%. Zhao et al. [6] proposed a method to identify vegetable diseases based on transfer learning and attention mechanisms; they proposed the DTL-SE-ResNet50 model to be able to identify diseases on vegetables; this model is integrated combined from ResNet50, SENet, and transfer learning models, this approach has brought accuracy up to 97.24% on two data sets: AI Challenger 2018 and self-built. Zhou et al. [7] proposed PRP-Net with the essential network structure ResNet18 and the extended network structure, achieving 98.26% accuracy in identifying plant diseases for complex backgrounds based on region proposal and progressive learning. This model locates regions of interest in diseased leaf images to conduct progressive learning in finer-scale networks. This is a good research direction because the model needs to learn images of the surrounding environment, not just parts of trees and monochrome backgrounds. The region recommendation part of this model can guide the model to focus on regions of interest in disease images. Yunyoung Nam [8] proposed a model with a combination of ONNX and tinyYOLOv2 models to locate the disease and then use EfficientNetb0 to extract features; this model produces an accuracy of 96.46% with the dataset PlantVillage. Sudau et al. [9] have compiled recent advances in optical imaging to detect diseases in fruits and vegetables. In that article, they have summarized many techniques on many types of optical images. Chen et al. [10] compared the performance of different lightning neural networks in different types of vegetables and fruits. They used six different models, including AlexNet, 18-layer ResNet, EfficientNet, and their respective pre-trained versions; the highest result belonged to pre-trained EfficientNet, whose metrics are superior to the remaining cases. Wang et al. [11] published Research on Intelligent Identification of Crop Pests and Diseases Based on the Improved YOLOv8 Model; the improvements include the use of GAM to weigh the vital feature information, improving the accuracy of the model. The RFA Conv method is used instead of standard convolution operations to enhance the ability to process feature information. Rehman et al. [12] proposed a method for apple leaf disease recognition with MASK RCNN and transfer learning, which provides a proposal for a model including AI step detection and classification in parallel; this model combines ResNet101 with FPN to create MASK RCNN and combines it with the transfer learning method. The result of this model is 96.6%. Zhang et al. [13] use an improved deep neural network to identify diseases on corn leaves; this study improves the network structure of GoogleLeNet and Cifar10, achieving results of 98.9% and 98.8%, respectively.

In addition, we will present more research related to more manual measures to prevent diseases on vegetables; for example, Thomas Pressecq et al. [14] surveyed with questions about the use of biological control products to analyze farmers' perspectives on disease control in vegetable production in France. Dedong Min et al. [15] analyzed the application of methyl jasmonate to control postharvest vegetable diseases; according to this review, methyl jasmonate can inhibit the development of postharvest vegetable diseases.

3   Material and Methods

3.1   Dataset

The dataset used to train the model is Cauliflower Dataset [16] this dataset provides field imagery where external factors can affect model accuracy but where it will be deployed in practice. This data set includes three types of diseases: downy mildew, black rot, and bacterial spot rot, which exist in each bed. In addition, images of disease-free cauliflower plants and 656 original images taken in a farmland environment are included. A brief overview of the data will be described in Table 1 and Fig. 1.

Table 1. Details of each class.

Class	Number of image
Bacterial spot rot	173
Black Rot	100
No Disease	206
Downy Mildew	177

(a) Bacterial Spot Rot.   (b) Black Rot.

(c) No Disease.   (d) Downy Mildew.

Fig. 1. Some illustrations of various classes in the considered dataset.

3.2   Preprocessing and Data Augmentation

The original image set's images are not the same size, so we resized them to a single size (224×224) to help the model learn better. Then, we apply image augmentation only to the training set to expand the data set and avoid overfitting. Our data augmentation methods include horizontal flip, rotation range, width shift range, height shift range, and zoom range. Some sample images after applying data augmentation are shown in Fig. 2

3.3   Image Identification Model for Cauliflower Diseases

The model uses the transfer learning method with EfficientNet and the stratified 5-Fold Cross Validation method to more generally evaluate the accuracy and

(a) After enhancement 1. (b) After enhancement 2. (c) After enhancement 3.

(d) The original image.

Fig. 2. An original image and its augmented images.

ensure that the data point is not misvalued because of some data points. The model can be described in pictorial form as Fig. 3.

The hyperparameters used for the model are shown in the Table 2.

Table 2. Hyperparameters were used.

Hyperparameters	Value
Learning rate	0.001
Epoch	15
Batch size	32
Optimizer	Adamax
Activation funtion	Relu

The reason we decided to use EfficientNet is because of the efficiency it brings; EfficientNet is a deep learning model designed to optimize performance with a low number of parameters, introduced by Tan et al. [17] in 2019. Some essential points that EfficientNet brings are that it uses a compound scaling strategy to increase network size instead of just increasing height, width, or resolution; EfficientNet increases both by the same ratio, which can limit computational

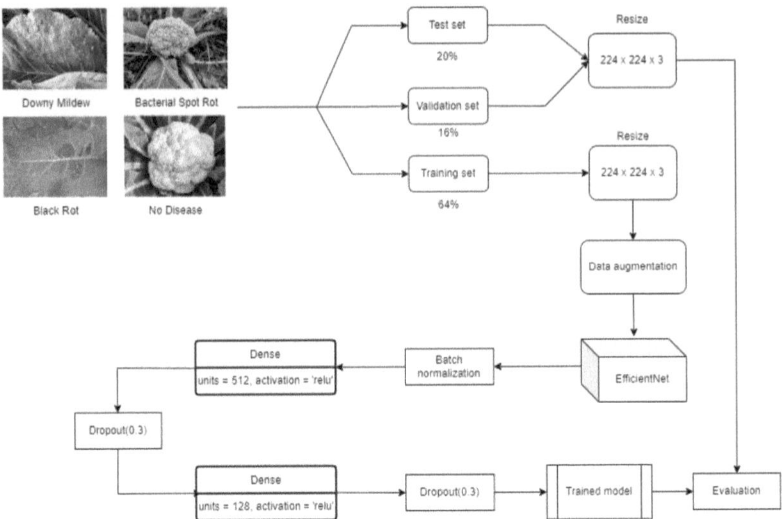

Fig. 3. The proposed EfficientNet for Vegetable disease diagnosis.

resources while still ensuring good performance. Versions of EfficientNet range from B0 to B7, and there is also an improved version called EfficientNetV2.

3.4   Environment Setting

The model training process is deployed on two different environments: Google Colab and Kaggle. The hardware parameters are described in the table below 3.

Table 3. Hardware device parameters

	Google Colab	Kaggle
GPU	T4	P100
RAM	12.7 GB	29 GB
GPU RAM	15 GB	16 GB
Disk	112.6 GB	57.6 GB

4   Experiments

4.1   Model Evaluation

This section will compare architectures' results with various metrics, including precision, recall, and f1-score, necessary to compare the results.

$$Precision = \frac{TP}{TP + FP} \tag{1}$$

Precision (Eq. 1) measures the ratio between the correct predictions of positive cases (affected by the disease), True Positive (TP), and that class's total number of predictions, including TP and False Positive (FP).

$$Recall = \frac{TP}{TP + FN} \tag{2}$$

Recall (Eq. 2) measures the ratio between the number of correct predictions belonging to the class of interest (TP) and the total number of actual numbers belonging to that class (TP + FN); recall measures the model's ability to identify all cases that belong to the class that needs attention.

$$F1 = 2 \cdot \frac{Precision \cdot Recall}{Precision + Recall} \tag{3}$$

F1-score (Eq. 3) helps evaluate the model's overall performance, especially in cases where the data is unbalanced between classes.

4.2 Results of Versions

In this section, our research uses a version of EfficientNet similar to the version that [5] uses, EfficientNet-B3. However, there are differences in the way the model is built, including layers, model configuration parameters, and model parameters, as well as data augmentation. In addition, we also use some other versions of EfficientNet to compare accuracy. The following confusion matrix is our proposed version of EfficientNet-B3 as shown in Fig. 4; the confusion matrix will show which labels the model misidentified, helping to determine directions for improvement and be used to compare models with each other.

The model identifies three types of diseases: Bacterial spot rot, downy mildew, and no disease. However, for black rot, there is a small quantity of confusion; this happens in all versions, not just B3. Although the number is not too large, this should be worth noting again. This could be because the number of images in the dataset is unbalanced. The number of images for each class participating in this evaluation is 35 with bacterial spot rot, 21 with black rot, 35 with downy mildew, and 42 with no disease, totaling 133 images, equal to 20% of the total number of images in the entire dataset; that is, there is only one wrong image out of a total of 133 images, the accuracy of the model we built with EfficientNet-B3 was 99.70% compared to 98% for Pradhan et al. [5]. Note that this cannot evaluate the entire model; it only gives us a general view of the classes. We have an accuracy chart as shown in Fig. 5, our classification report for usage model B3 is shown in the following Table 5, and the loss and precision are shown in Fig. 6, overall, our model is somewhat superior to their model as the indexes are higher. Our model's accuracy is the average of five models generated from the stratified 5-Fold Cross Validation method. The table showing the accuracy and standard deviation is shown in the following Table 4.

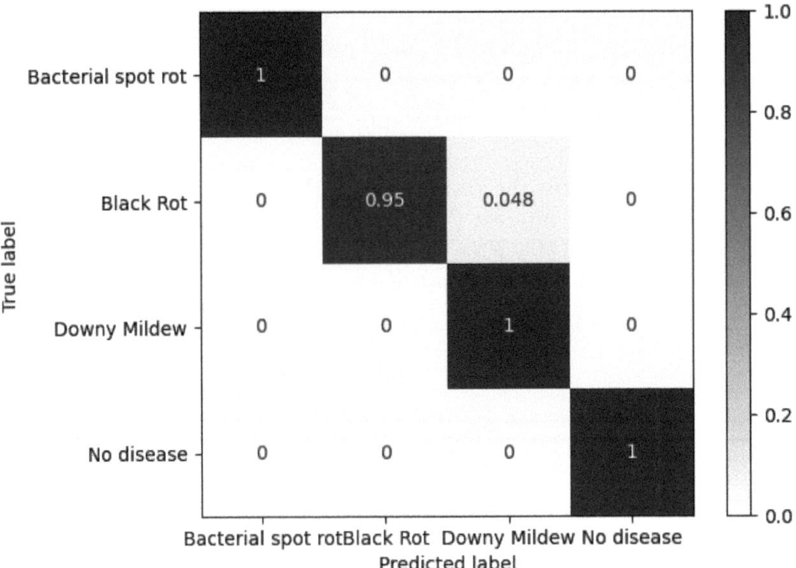

Fig. 4. An illustration of the normalized confusion matrix of EfficientNet-B3 on a fold.

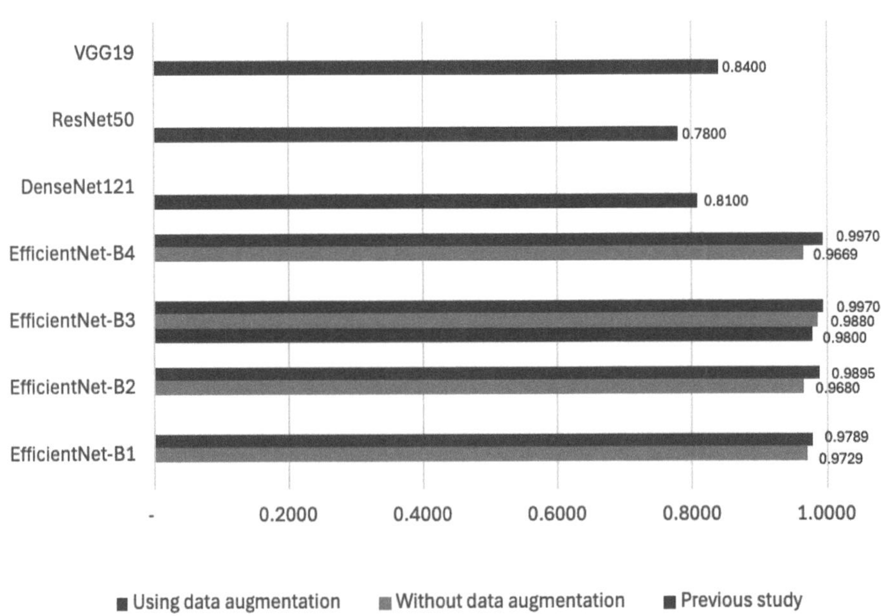

Fig. 5. Results comparison with a previous study [5].

Table 4. The average accuracy and standard deviation on the original dataset.

Model	Using data augmentation	Without data augmentation
EfficientNet-B1	0.9789 ± 0.0110	0.9729 ± 0.0090
EfficientNet-B2	0.9789 ± 0.0160	0.9729 ± 0.0122
EfficientNet-B3	0.9970 ± 0.0060	0.9880 ± 0.0076
EfficientNet-B4	0.9970 ± 0.0060	0.9669 ± 0.0095

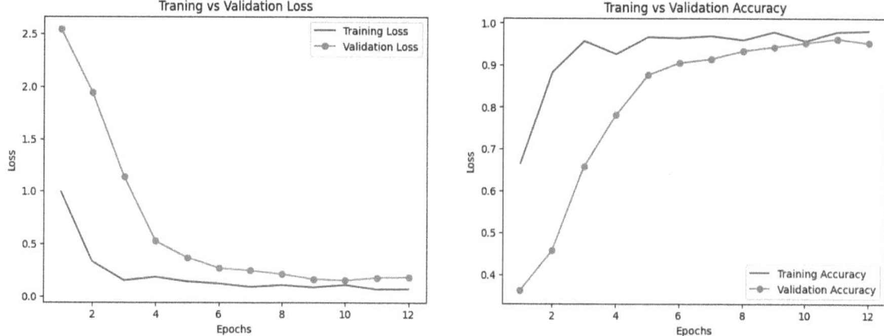

Fig. 6. Loss and accuracy during the learning with EfficientNetB3.

4.3   Imbalanced Data

To solve this data imbalance problem, we use two different methods: reduce the dataset so that the number of images in the classes is equal (Undersampling) and the second way is to add augmented images to the layers with a low number of images to be equal to the layer with the most significant number of images.

Undersampling. This method only reduces images on the training set, not the original data set. For each version, we run it once without image enhancement and once using the image enhancement technique mentioned above. The results

Table 5. Classification report of EfficientNet-B3.

	Precision	Recall	F1-score
Bacterial Spot Rot	1.00	1.00	1.00
Black Rot	1.00	0.95	0.98
Downy Mildew	0.97	1.00	0.99
No Disease	1.00	1.00	1.00
Macro Average	0.99	0.99	0.99
Weighted Average	0.99	0.99	0.99

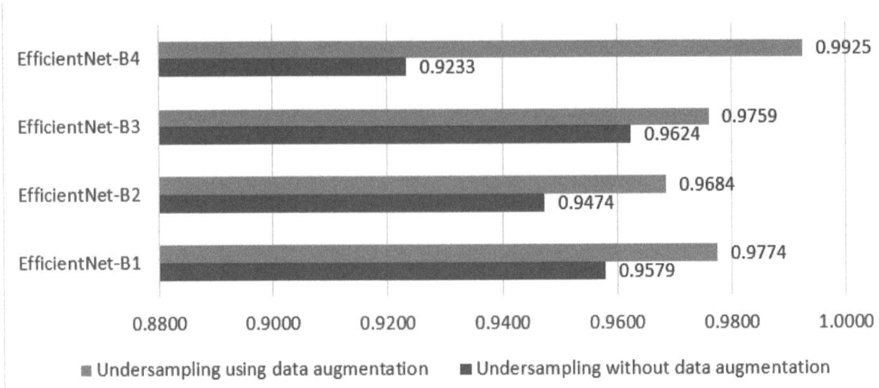

Fig. 7. Chart comparing the results of the undersampling method.

Table 6. The average accuracy and standard deviation with undersampling method.

Model	Undersampling and using data augmentation	Undersampling and without data augmentation
EfficientNet-B1	0.9774 ± 0.0142	0.9579 ± 0.0632
EfficientNet-B2	0.9684 ± 0.0257	0.9474 ± 0.0349
EfficientNet-B3	0.9759 ± 0.0198	0.9624 ± 0.0195
EfficientNet-B4	0.9925 ± 0.0082	0.9233 ± 0.0203

are shown in the following Fig. 7. The table showing the accuracy and standard deviation is shown in the following Table 6

It can be seen that the accuracy has decreased in all models. This may be due to the number of images on the training set often being reduced by 42 to 44%; reducing too large of images makes the model Confused when identifying classes, causing accuracy to decrease.

Enhance Minority Class Image. With this method, we make the classes in the dataset have the same number of images by adding augmented images to the minority classes; here, we add images after the dataset splitting stage, which means we will have two times of data augmentation: the first time is to solve the image imbalance and the second time is to increase the number of images in the whole set. The methods we use for the first enhancement include brightness, vertical flip, and shear. The results are shown in the following Fig. 8. The table showing the accuracy and standard deviation is in the following Table 7.

Looking at the chart above, we can see that this method increased the model's accuracy slightly in the low versions but remained the same at B4, indicating that this may have been the model's maximum or the real problem does not just come from imbalance. In addition, when using this method, we ran it on a different way of dividing the data: using 5-Fold from the beginning, which will increase the training set to 80% and the test set will be 20%. Overall, our

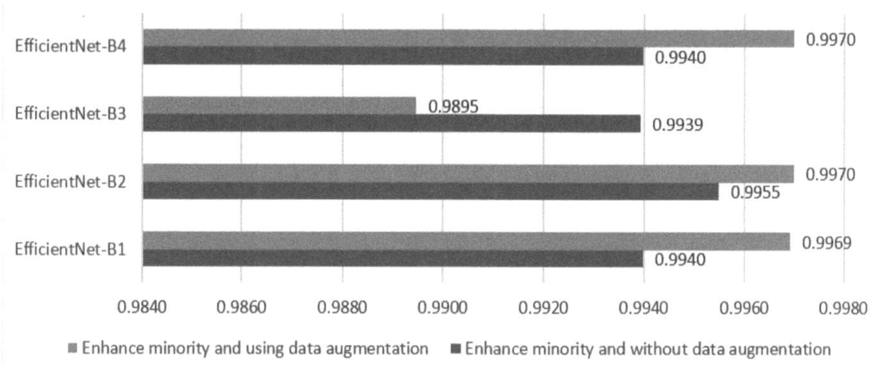

Fig. 8. Chart comparing the results of the enhanced minority method.

Table 7. The average accuracy and standard deviation of enhance minority method.

Model	Enhance minority and using data augmentation	Enhance minority and without data augmentation
EfficientNet-B1	0.9969 ± 0.0037	0.9939 ± 0.003
EfficientNet-B2	0.9970 ± 0.006	0.9955 ± 0.009
EfficientNet-B3	0.9895 ± 0.0076	0.9939 ± 0.003
EfficientNet-B4	0.9970 ± 0.006	0.9940 ± 0.003

model is still very good. The results are compared with [5] previous study and are shown in the following Fig. 9. The table showing the accuracy and standard deviation is in the following Table 8.

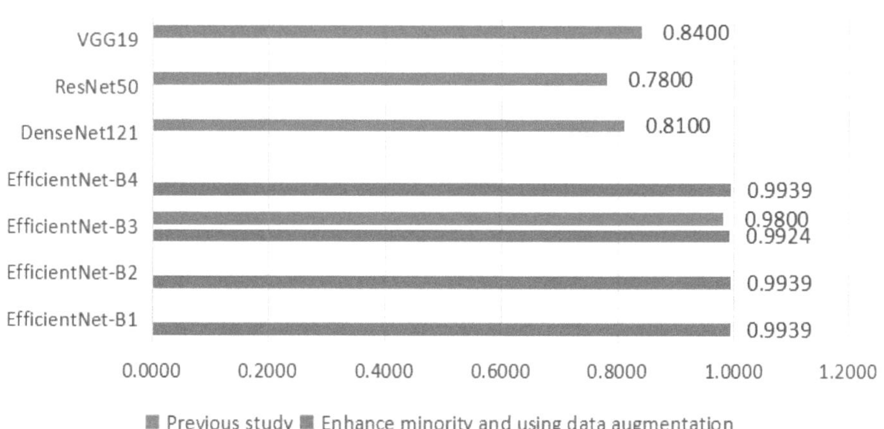

Fig. 9. Chart comparing the results of the enhanced minority method and 80–20 dataset split with the previous study [5].

Table 8. The average accuracy and standard deviation of the enhanced minority method with 80–20 dataset split.

Model	Using enhanced minority and 80–20 dataset split
EfficientNet-B1	0.9939 ± 0.0056
EfficientNet-B2	0.9939 ± 0.0056
EfficientNet-B3	0.9924 ± 0.0048
EfficientNet-B4	0.9939 ± 0.0056

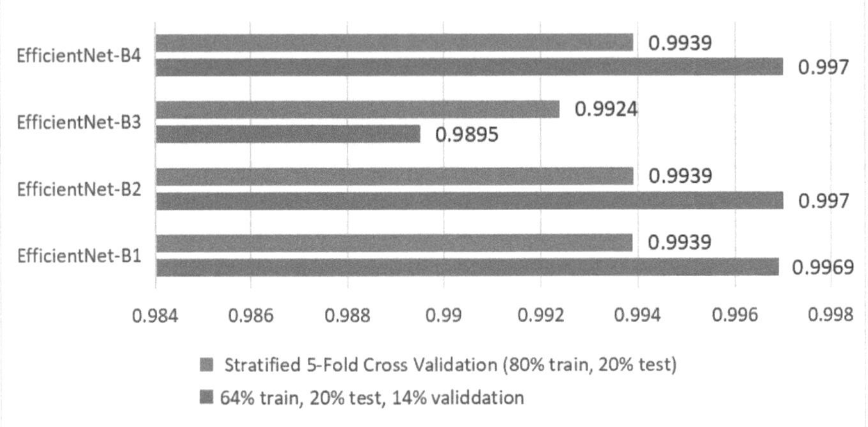

Fig. 10. Comparison chart of two ways of splitting the data set.

Here, we also make a comparison chart of the results of the two ways of splitting the dataset using the same method: enhancing minority class image and using data augmentation. The results are compared shown in the following Fig. 10.

5   Conclusion

EfficientNet is a practical approach for distinguishing plant diseases with relatively high accuracy compared to other network architectures. In the scope of this article, we only use a small architecture of EfficientNet, which is B1, B2, B3, and B4. In addition, EfficientNet has other versions stretching from B0 to B7 and versions of EfficientNetv2; of course, more significant is only sometimes better as we may have to trade time because the number of parameters apart is quite large, which entails risks. We hope the proposed model can contribute to reducing the cauliflower epidemic, partly solving the global food shortage, and contributing to future readers' research.

In the future, we hope to be able to improve the data, increase the number of diseases at an earlier detection level so that they can be prevented as early as possible, and add images from many varieties of cauliflower at many times at different points of the day and locations to enable early deployment in a field environment so that the model can identify diseases in more vegetables.

Data Availability Statement. The data supporting this study's findings are available at [16].

References

1. Jideani, A.I.O., Silungwe, H., Takalani, T., Omolola, A.O., Udeh, H.O., Anyasi, T.A.: Antioxidant-rich natural fruit and vegetable products and human health. Int. J. Food Properties **24**(1), 41–67 (2021). http://dx.doi.org/10.1080/10942912.2020.1866597
2. dos Reis, L.C.R., de Oliveira, V.R., Hagen, M.E.K., Jablonski, A., Flôres, S.H., de Oliveira Rios, A.: Carotenoids, flavonoids, chlorophylls, phenolic compounds and antioxidant activity in fresh and cooked broccoli (brassica oleracea var. avenger) and cauliflower (brassica oleracea var. alphina f1). LWT - Food Sci. Technol. **63**(1), 177–183 (2015). http://dx.doi.org/10.1016/j.lwt.2015.03.089
3. Khayitovna, P.M., Faxriddinovich, M.S.: Peculiarities of growing cauliflower (2022)
4. Sun, W., et al.: Dfyolov5m-m2transformer: interpretation of vegetable disease recognition results using image dense captioning techniques. Comput. Electron. Agri. **215**, 108460 (2023). http://dx.doi.org/10.1016/j.compag.2023.108460
5. Pradhan, N.R., Ghosh, H., Rahat, I.S., Naga Ramesh, J.V., Yesubabu, M.: Enhancing agricultural sustainability with deep learning: a case study of cauliflower disease classification. EAI Endorsed Trans. Internet Things **10** (2024). http://dx.doi.org/10.4108/eetiot.4834
6. Zhao, X., Li, K., Li, Y., Ma, J., Zhang, L.: Identification method of vegetable diseases based on transfer learning and attention mechanism. Comput. Electron. Agri. **193**, 106703 (2022). http://dx.doi.org/10.1016/j.compag.2022.106703
7. Zhou, J., Li, J., Wang, C., Wu, H., Zhao, C., Wang, Q.: A vegetable disease recognition model for complex background based on region proposal and progressive learning. Comput. Electron. Agri. **184**, 106101 (2021). https://doi.org/10.1016/j.compag.2021.106101
8. Amin, J., Almas Anjum, M., Sharif, M., Kadry, S., Nam, Y.: Fruits and vegetable diseases recognition using convolutional neural networks. Comput. Mater. Contin. **70**(1), 619–635 (2022)
9. Eh Teet, S., Hashim, N.: Recent advances of application of optical imaging techniques for disease detection in fruits and vegetables: a review. Food Control **152**, 109849 (2023). http://dx.doi.org/10.1016/j.foodcont.2023.109849
10. Chen, Y., Pan, S., Wang, H.: Performance comparison of different convolutional neural networks for vegetable and fruit recognition. Appl. Comput. Eng. **5**(1), 593–602 (2023). http://dx.doi.org/10.54254/2755-2721/5/20230652
11. Wang, Y., Yi, C., Huang, T., Liu, J.: Research on intelligent recognition for plant pests and diseases based on improved yolov8 model. Appl. Sci. **14**(12), 5353 (2024). http://dx.doi.org/10.3390/app14125353
12. Rehman, Z.u., et al.: Recognizing apple leaf diseases using a novel parallel real-time processing framework based on mask RCNN and transfer learning: an application for smart agriculture. IET Image Process. **15**(10), 2157–2168 (2021). http://dx.doi.org/10.1049/ipr2.12183

13. Zhang, X., Qiao, Y., Meng, F., Fan, C., Zhang, M.: Identification of maize leaf diseases using improved deep convolutional neural networks. IEEE Access **6**, 30370–30377 (2018). http://dx.doi.org/10.1109/ACCESS.2018.2844405
14. Pressecq, T., et al.: Using microbial biocontrol for disease control in French vegetable production: an analysis of the perspectives of farmers and farm advisors. Crop Prot. **180**, 106648 (2024). http://dx.doi.org/10.1016/j.cropro.2024.106648
15. Min, D., Li, F., Ali, M., Zhang, X., Liu, Y.: Application of methyl Jasmonate to control disease of postharvest fruit and vegetables: a meta-analysis. Postharvest Biol. Technol. **208**, 112667 (2024). http://dx.doi.org/10.1016/j.postharvbio.2023.112667
16. Rajbongshi, A.: VegNet: an extensive dataset of cauliflower images to recognize the diseases using machine learning and deep learning models (2022). https://data.mendeley.com/datasets/t5sssfgn2v/3
17. Tan, M., Le, Q.V.: EfficientNet: rethinking model scaling for convolutional neural networks (2019). https://arxiv.org/abs/1905.11946

Rice Varieties Classification Combining Scalers and Fine-Tuned Classical Machine Learning

Hai Thanh Nguyen[1], Phat Tuan Hong Nguyen[2], and Anh Kim Su[2(✉)]

[1] College of Information and Communication Technology, Can Tho University, Can Tho, Vietnam
nthai.cit@ctu.edu.vn
[2] College of Rural Development, Can Tho University, Can Tho, Vietnam
phatb2111894@student.ctu.edu.vn, sukimanh@ctu.edu.vn

Abstract. Rice is the most essential food crop and contributes to agricultural economic development in Vietnam. With climate changes, accurate classification of rice types is essential to ensure food security and recognize the rice quality. Leveraging Fine-tuned Classical Machine Learning, this study focuses on two rice varieties: Osmancik and Cameo. The classification processing conducted data preprocessing and used GridSearchCV to indicate the best hyperparameters for some classical algorithms. Results showed that the SVM algorithm obtained 92.94% accuracy in classifying the above two rice varieties. Accurate identification of rice varieties through fine-tuning parameters ensures precision in rice assessment and grading, meets different consumer needs and promotes innovation in cultivation and rice processing. This research promotes the application of artificial intelligence problems in classifying agricultural products, supporting agricultural economic development, and classifying crops in agriculture.

Keywords: rice classification · varieties · classical machine learning · fine-tuned hyper-parameters

1 Introduction

AI applications in agriculture are gaining popularity because of their ability to evaluate and are cheaper than manual methods [1]. AI offers more significant benefits than manual methods [2]. Research [3] shows that manual analysis and classification of rice is time-consuming and costly due to human variables. The evaluation process can vary depending on the manual method because the reviewers' experience differs. Additionally, making quick decisions on a large scale is a challenge of manual methods. The authors in [4] asserted that rice, a globally produced and consumed cereal, was valued based on various parameters in the market, such as roughness, shape, color, and crack ratio. After obtaining the rice features, various machine learning algorithms could be used to determine

© ICST Institute for Computer Sciences, Social Informatics and Telecommunications Engineering 2026
Published by Springer Nature Switzerland AG 2026. All Rights Reserved
P. Cong Vinh et al. (Eds.): ICTCC 2024, LNICST 668, pp. 15–26, 2026.
https://doi.org/10.1007/978-3-032-12846-1_2

these parameters and aim to perform classification tasks for comparison. Using such methods in rice production was essential to improve the quality of the final product and meet food safety criteria in an automatic, economical, and efficient manner [5–7].

Recently, many feature datasets have been used to evaluate rice classification and quality. These features include geometric parameters (area, perimeter, etc.), crack ratio, whiteness, and identifying rice grain cracks. Image processing-based systems can extract various features of grain products. Moreover, these features are classified using techniques such as Artificial Neural Networks (ANN) and Support Vector Machines (SVM), Logistic Regression (LR), Deep Neural Networks (DNN), and Convolutional Neural Networks (CNN) from machine learning algorithms.

This study aims to indicate a practical algorithm that helps create a robust model to improve classification using feature datasets from different rice varieties. We improved the algorithm's accuracy through detailed data preprocessing and finding the best hyperparameters for each algorithm, which previous authors should have done. The work is expected to be the pre-treatment step that has helped classify and evaluate the quality of rice grains more effectively to provide a tool for intelligent agriculture.

2   Related Work

In [8], authors used a Deep Convolutional Neural Network (DCNN) to classify rice plants and obtained a good accuracy of 95.50%. They demonstrated the effectiveness of DCNN in rice classification by leveraging unique features obtained from the data. Another study [9] used a test dataset of 200 samples from 16 classes and achieved an accuracy of 87.16% using the SVM algorithm. Furthermore, in another research effort using three rice varieties and 200 data samples, researchers applied CNN for the classification method after feature extraction, achieving a success rate of 88.07% [10]. In 2019, Cinar et al. in [11] implemented a Support Vector Machine (SVM) to classify rice varieties with 92.83%

In the study in [12], the authors performed the wheat classification and achieved an impressive accuracy of 95.90% using a Support Vector Machine (SVM). This success was achieved using 4,366 samples and five features, effectively demonstrating the applicability of SVM in agricultural classification applications. Ebrahimi et al. (2014) [13] explored wheat classification using Artificial Neural Network (ANN) to classify between various wheat varieties using 640 samples and two traits, they achieved 87.50%

In addition, another study [14] delved into wheat classification. They focused mainly on SVM on 7,000 samples and two features; this study achieved an accuracy of 86.81%. The successful classification of wheat varieties through SVM in this study has contributed valuable insights to the field of agricultural research. In their study [15], they performed experiments using the Support Vector Machine (SVM) to classify wheat varieties based on multiple characteristics. Their study, using 6,400 samples and 40 features, achieved an accuracy of 88.33%. By leveraging SVM, the effectiveness of the classification model was proven in accurately identifying wheat varieties. The study [16] conducted a comprehensive study on dry bean classification using a Support Vector Machine (SVM) to classify dry bean varieties based on multiple characteristics. Using a dataset of 13,611 samples and seven features, their study achieved 93.13% accuracy. Through SVM, they demonstrate the effectiveness of the classification model in accurately identifying dry beans. Table 1 outlines some earlier studies.

Table 1. Some previous studies on rice variance classification.

Crop	Data Pieces	Class	Accuracy	Classifier	References
Rice	7,399	3	95.50%	DCNN	[8]
Rice	3,810	2	92.83%	SVM	[11]
Rice	200	3	88.07%	CNN	[10]
Rice	200	16	87.16%	SVM	[9]
Wheat	640	2	87.50%	ANN	[13]
Wheat	6,400	40	88.33%	SVM	[15]
Wheat	3,000	2	93.46%	ANN	[17]
Wheat	180	2	95.00%	SVM	[18]
Wheat	7,000	2	86.81%	SVM	[14]
Wheat	150	16	72.80%	ANN	[19]
Wheat	4,366	5	95.90%	SVM	[12]
Drybean	13,611	7	93.13%	SVM	[16]
Soybean	200	2	99.93%	ANN	[20]

3 Methodology

3.1 Rice Dataset

We used a quality features dataset for the study, obtained from Ilkay Cinar [11]. Seven features for each grain are total. The features and explanations used in feature extracts for both types of rice are given in [11] with 2180 Osmancik samples and 1630 Cameo samples, as presented in Table 2. The minimum, average, maximum, and standard deviation data for both types of rice samples are given in Table 3. The histogram is presented in Fig. 1.

Using our algorithms, we tested the results with datasets from research papers in Table 1 during the reference process. Data sets found from research papers: [11, 16, 17] (being compared in the results). The dataset [17] has 9,000 data; each has 236 attributes and belongs to 1 of 3 classes. In the data set [16], there are 13,611 data of 7 different types of dry beans, 16 attributes of which 12 are size attributes, and 4 are shape attributes from the beans. However, some remaining studies: [8–10, 12–15, 18–21] do not is there a willingness to share datasets so we cannot run experiments.

Table 2. Features and explanations used in feature extraction

Name	Explanation
Area	Returns the number of pixels inside the limits of Rice grain.
Perimeter	The circumference of rice grains is calculated by measuring the distance between pixels around their edges.
MajorAxisLength	The longest line drawn on the rice grain is also known as the central axis distance.
MinorAxisLength	Refers to the shortest line on the rice grain, also known as the small axis distance.
Eccentricity	The ellipse's roundness is measured using the same moments as a rice grain.
Convex Area	This function returns the pixel count of the smallest convex shell in the rice grain region.
Extent	Returns the ratio of rice grain region to bounding box pixels.

Table 3. Descriptive statistics of rice species data

Features	Min	Mean	Max	Std. Dev.
Area	7551.0000	12667.7276	18913.0000	1732.3677
Perimeter	359.1000	454.2392	548.4460	35.5971
MajorAxisLength	145.2645	188.7762	239.0105	17.44870
MinorAxisLength	59.5324	86.3138	107.5424	5.7298
Eccentricity	0.7772	0.8869	0.9480	0.0208
ConvexArea	7723.0000	12952.4969	19099.0000	1776.9720
Extent	0.4974	0.6619	0.8610	0.0772

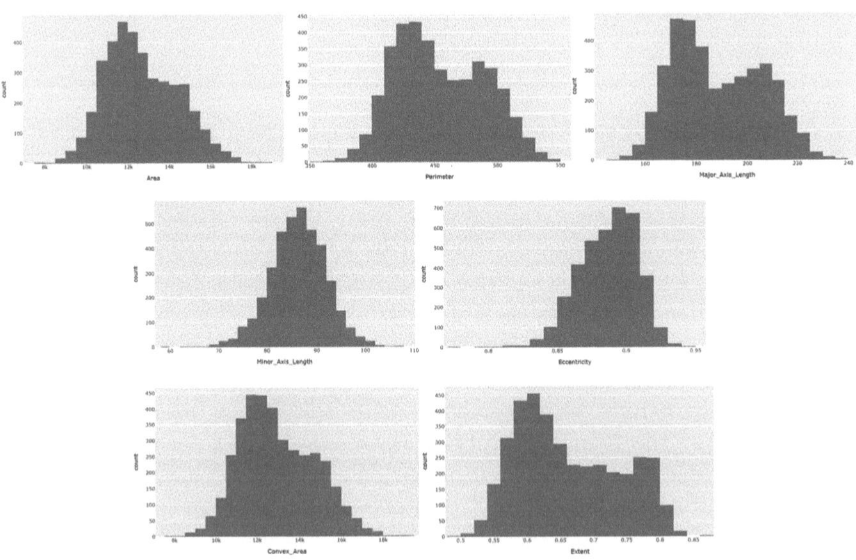

Fig. 1. Histograms of Features Before Scaling.

3.2   Pre-proccesing Rice Features Dataset

Before beginning the classification process, the feature datasets for rice varieties are standardized using a technique known as "Scaler". Scaler is a data normalization technique that ensures features have similar value ranges. This can lead to allow the classification model to perform more effectively. This procedure can be required in the case the features of rice data can vary in magnitude and value range. Failure to normalize may cause the model to be influenced by features with larger or smaller value ranges, resulting in difficulties with learning, optimization, or reduced model performance. Scalers can normalize features using scaling, such as normalization (z-point normalization) or Min-Max conversions to ensure that the features can have the same scale and range of value, facilitating classification model learning and improving predictability. We conducted a test run and compared the above two scaler methods. Then, we choose to use the MinMaxScaler (Min-Max conversion). After the Min-Max transformation, the descriptive statistics of rice species data may show a more consistent scale and distribution across different features, as shown in Table 4.

Table 4. Statistics describing rice species data after normalization

Features	Min	Mean	Max	Std. Dev.
Area	0	0.4503	1.0000	0.1525
Perimeter	0	0.5025	1.0000	0.1880
MajorAxisLength	0	0.4641	1.0000	0.1861
MinorAxisLength	0	0.5578	1.0000	0.1193
Eccentricity	0	0.6420	1.0000	0.1219
ConvexArea	0	0.4597	1.0000	0.1562
Extent	0	0.4524	1.0000	0.2124

3.3   Algorithms for Classification

In this research work, we use the scikit-learn library's GridSearchCV to determine the hyperparameter set with the maximum accuracy score that GridSearchCV achieves when looking for a grid of hyperparameters. The grid of hyperparameters will be proposed differently, depending on the algorithms. The proposed algorithms are k-NN, NB, RF, DT, SVM, XGB, LR, Bagging DT, and Bagging k-NN. We choose these algorithms to create diversity and possibilities, efficient data processing, simplicity, tunability, and the ability to integrate and compare performance to achieve the best classification results for a 3810 dataset, seven features, and two classes.

K-Nearest Neighbors (k-NN) predicts the class of a new data point by considering the classes of its k nearest neighbors in the feature space. In our study, we proposed the following grid of hyperparameters for the algorithm: n_neighbors ranging from 1 to 9, weights as either 'uniform' or 'distance,' algorithm as one of 'auto,' 'ball_tree,' 'kd_tree,' or 'brute,' and p as either 1 or 2. We selected the following hyperparameters for the model because they achieved the highest accuracy score during the GridSearchCV: algorithm set to 'auto', leaf_size set to 30, metric as 'minkowski', metric_params as None, n_jobs as None, n_neighbors set to 8, p set to 1, and weights set to 'uniform'.

Naive Bayes (NB) can perform well on many classification tasks, especially when dealing with high-dimensional datasets. In our experiments, we used the algorithm's default hyperparameters.

Random Forest (RF) can effectively handle missing values and perform well even with many input variables. In our study, we proposed the following grid of hyperparameters for the algorithm: n_estimators with values [100, 200, 300], criterion as either 'gini' or 'entropy', max_depth with values [None, 10, 20, 30], min_samples_split with values [2, 5, 10], min_samples_leaf with values [1, 2, 4], and bootstrap as either True or False. We chose the following hyperparameters for the algorithm because they yielded the best results during GridSearchCV: n_estimators set to 300, criterion set to 'gini', max_depth set to 10, min_samples_split set to 5, min_samples_leaf set to 1, and bootstrap set to True. **Decision Tree (DT)** is a simple and interpretable algorithm that recursively splits the considered data into subsets at each node based on the most significant attribute. For our study, we used the following hyperparameter grid for the algorithm: criterion as either 'gini' or 'entropy', max_depth with values [5, 10, 15, 20, 25, 30, None], min_samples_split with values [2, 5, 10, 15, 20], and min_samples_leaf with values [1, 2, 4, 6, 8, 10]. The best parameters found by GridSearchCV for the algorithm were: criterion set to 'entropy', max_depth set to 5, min_samples_leaf set to 6, and min_samples_split set to 2. **Extreme Gradient Boosting (XGB)**, namely XGBoost, can be considered an efficient and scalable implementation of gradient boosting algorithms. However, tuning the hyperparameters can be challenging, and we are facing a long training time that may be longer than other algorithms. Our study used the following hyperparameter grid for the algorithm: n_estimators with values ranging from 100 to 900 in steps of 100, max_depth with values ranging from 3 to 9, gamma with values ranging from 0 to 0.4 in steps of 0.1, and reg_alpha with values [0, 0.0001, 0.001, 0.01, 0.1]. Following the grid search, we chose the optimal parameters: n_estimators set to 100, max_depth set to 3, gamma set to 0.4, and reg_alpha set to 0.01. **Bootstrap Aggregating (Bagging)**, also known as bagging, decreases variance and helps to mitigate overfitting by averaging or voting on individual model predictions. It efficiently lowers the effects of data noise and outliers while improving poor learners' generalization performance. Bagging integrates with various basic models, including decision trees and neural networks. However, if the underlying models are strongly coupled or the dataset is intrinsically noisy, it may result in insignificant gains. With BaggingDT and BaggingkNN, we reuse the best parameters of the previous DT and k-NN algorithms; the number of decision trees - 'n_estimators' selected is 10.

Support Vector Machine (SVM) is a robust supervised learning algorithm for classification and regression tasks. SVM has a regularization parameter that helps control overfitting. In our investigation, we used the following hyperparameter grid for the SVM algorithm: C with values [0.1, 1, 10, 100, 1000, 10000], kernel as 'linear', 'poly', 'rbf', or 'sigmoid', and gamma values ['scale', 'auto', 0.001, 0.01, 0.1, 1]. GridSearchCV determined that the optimal parameters for the SVM method were C = 10000, kernel = 'linear', and gamma = 0.01.

Logistic Regression (LR) can handle both numeric and categorical characteristics and can be used for multi-class classification with one-on-one or polynomial techniques. For Logistic Regression (LR), we used the algorithm's default hyperparameters.

4 Experiments

4.1 Environment Setup

We processed and classified objects in a Visual Studio Code environment with an NVIDIA GeForce RTX 3050 Ti Laptop GPU, which has 2560 CUDA (Compute Unified Device Architecture) cores, 16GB DDR4 RAM, and an Intel i7-11800H 2.3GHz CPU. The algorithms were compiled and executed in Python, version 3.11.6. To conduct the model training, we divided it into a training set and a test set in a ratio of 8:2 (3048 train, 762 test).

4.2 Results

Table 5 shows our algorithms' best experimental run results with two datasets [11, 16].

Table 5. Test results with reference datasets

Reference	Classifier	Accuracy	Precision	Recall	F1-score
[11]	k-NN	0.9887 ($\pm$0.0142)	0.9887 ($\pm$0.0142)	0.9887 ($\pm$0.0142)	0.9887 ($\pm$0.0142)
[16]	XGB	0.8401 ($\pm$0.3057)	0.8721 ($\pm$0.2206)	0.8401 ($\pm$0.3057)	0.8264 ($\pm$0.3407)

Figure 2 shows the results of comparing algorithms between scalers using acccuracy.

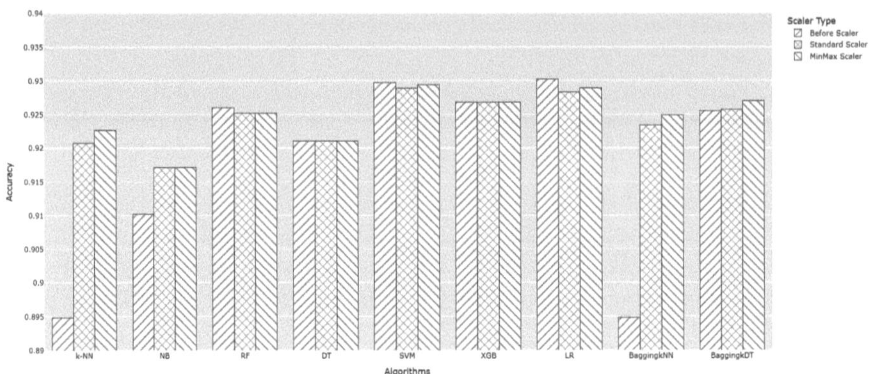

Fig. 2. Comparing the results of algorithms with different scalers.

Models have been trained, and their performances have been evaluated using k-NN, NB, RF, DT, SVM, XGB, LR, and Bagging machine learning techniques for classification. A cross-validation k value of 5 has been selected for all the models. Figure 3 presents the normalized confusion matrix values for all the algorithms used.

For classification performance metrics, success criteria such as Accuracy, Precision, Recall, and F1-Score are calculated using a normalized confusion matrix for each model. Table 6 gives classification performance measurement results.

Table 6. Results of classification performance

Algorithms	Accuracy	Precision	Recall	F1-score
k-NN	0.9226 (±0.0366)	0.9388 (±0.0419)	0.9252 (±0.0233)	0.9319 (±0.0313)
NB	0.9171 (±0.0501)	0.9228 (±0.0533)	0.9335 (±0.0314)	0.9281 (±0.0423)
RF	0.9252 (±0.0379)	0.9295 (±0.0475)	0.9394 (±0.0224)	0.9355 (±0.0330)
DT	0.9210 (±0.0394)	0.9279 (±0.0602)	0.9358 (±0.0126)	0.9315 (±0.0314)
SVM	0.9294 (±0.0338)	0.9359 (±0.0375)	0.9413 (±0.0254)	0.9385 (±0.0288)
XGB	0.9268 (±0.0449)	0.9326 (±0.0503)	0.9404 (±0.0287)	0.9364 (±0.0380)
LR	0.9289 (±0.0377)	0.9347 (±0.0450)	0.9376 (±0.0283)	0.9338 (±0.0353)
BaggingDT	0.9270 (±0.0350)	0.9309 (±0.0468)	0.9413 (±0.0147)	0.9358 (±0.0344)
BaggingkNN	0.9249 (±0.0397)	0.9302 (±0.0450)	0.9376 (±0.0283)	0.9356 (±0.0352)

As shown in Table 6, the NB and DT models have lower accuracy than the other models, with 91.71% and 92.10%, respectively. The Precision, Recall, and F1 indexes are also lower, showing that these two models have yet to reach their peak performance. This result could be due to the poor fit of the NB and DT models to the data or other factors, such as the model's dependence on specific hyper-parameters. The kNN, RF, XGB, and BaggingkNN models showed

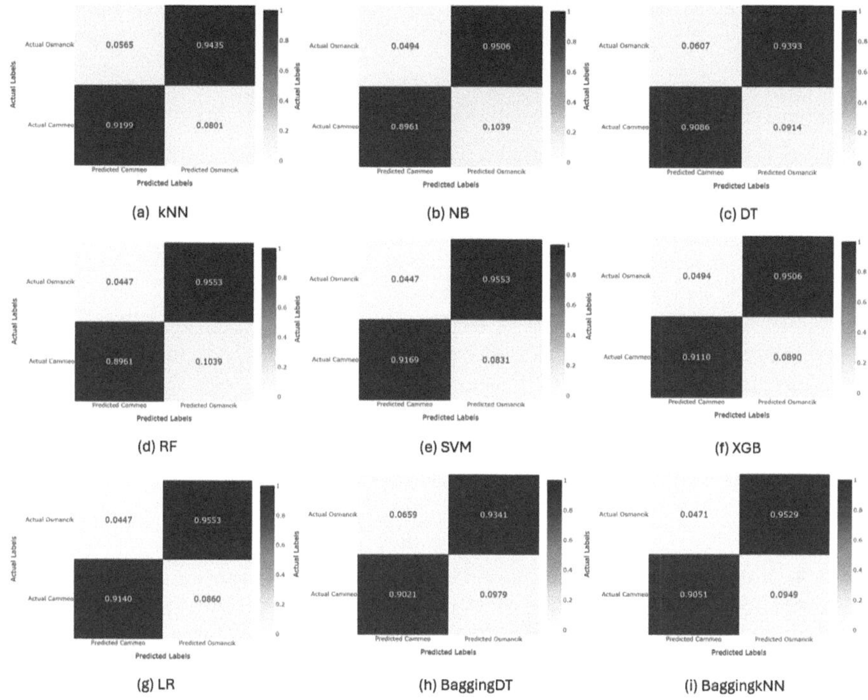

Fig. 3. Normalized confusion matrix of the algorithms used.

good classification ability with accuracy ranging from 92.26% to 92.68%. Ensemble models like RF and BaggingkNN are generally better able to generalize than single models like DT; the high RF recall rate of 93.94% shows its effectiveness in identifying favorable combinations of fields. Ensemble methods minimize the risk of individual model bias and bias, leading to more robust overall performance. With accuracy ranging from 92.70% to 92.94%, SVM, BaggingDT, and LR models give the best performance compared to other models. The SVM and LR models showed the highest recall rates of 94.13% and 94.17%, respectively, meaning they were particularly effective in obtaining true positives. However, this often comes at a small cost in terms of accuracy. Table 7 compared classification performance; the BaggingDT, SVM, and LR algorithms achieved equivalent accuracy on the Cinar Dataset, with slight variations in performance indicated by the benchmark scores. The BaggingDT (Fine-tuned) and SVM (Fine-tuned) models have higher accuracy than the untuned versions, as seen in the BaggingDT model, which jumped in accuracy from 91.31% to 92.70%, demonstrating the importance of hyperparameter optimization. The study's MLP, SVM, and DT models [11] achieved accuracy from 92.49% to 92.86%, which is very close to our results. This result highlights that our SVM model and other Fine-tuned models can provide comparable or better performance than those reported in previous research.

Table 7. Comparison of results with previous experiments

Algorithms	Accuracy	Dataset	References
BaggingDT (default hyperparameters)	0.9131 (±0.0337)	Cinar Dataset	Ours
BaggingDT (Fine-Tuned)	0.9270 (±0.0350)	Cinar Dataset	Ours
SVM (default hyperparameters)	0.9294 (±0.0361)	Cinar Dataset	Ours
SVM(Fine-Tuned)	0.9294 (±0.0338)	Cinar Dataset	Ours
LR (default hyperparameters)	0.9289 (±0.0377)	Cinar Dataset	Ours
MLP	0.9286	Cinar Dataset	[11]
SVM	0.9283	Cinar Dataset	[11]
DT	0.9249	Cinar Dataset	[11]

5   Conclusion

BaggingDT, SVM, and LR achieved the best accuracy, precision, recall, and F1 scores among the tested algorithms. BaggingDT achieved 92.70% accuracy, with Precision, Recall, and F1 scores above 93%. LR achieved high performance with an accuracy of 92.89%, with Precision, Recall, and F1 scores above 93%. SVM achieved high performance with an accuracy of 92.94%, with Precision, Recall, and F1 scores above 93%. This result shows that all three methods can predict particle type well, and LR and SVM have excellent stability, especially when handling non-linear data.

In the future, we will continue to research advanced hyperparameter optimization methods such as Bayesian Optimization, Stochastic Search, and Genetic Algorithms to find the best configurations for models. We will specifically focus on fine-tuning complex models such as XGB, SVM, and ensemble models to further improve performance.

References

1. Mahajan, S., Das, A., Sardana, H.K.: Image acquisition techniques for assessment of legume quality. Trends Food Sci. Technol. **42**(2), 116–133 (2015). https://doi.org/10.1016/j.tifs.2015.01.001
2. Barbedo, J.G.A.: A review on the main challenges in automatic plant disease identification based on visible range images. Biosyst. Eng. **144**, 52–60 (2016). http://dx.doi.org/10.1016/j.biosystemseng.2016.01.017
3. Patrício, D.I., Rieder, R.: Computer vision and artificial intelligence in precision agriculture for grain crops: a systematic review. Comput. Electron. Agri. **153**, 69–81 (2018). https://doi.org/10.1016/j.compag.2018.08.001
4. Aukkapinyo, K., Sawangwong, S., Pooyoi, P., Kusakunniran, W.: Localization and classification of rice-grain images using region proposals-based convolutional neural network. Int. J. Autom. Comput. **17**(2), 233–246 (2019). https://doi.org/10.1007/s11633-019-1207-6

5. Al-Jarrah, O.Y., Yoo, P.D., Muhaidat, S., Karagiannidis, G.K., Taha, K.: Efficient machine learning for big data: a review. Big Data Res. **2**(3), 87–93 (2015). http://dx.doi.org/10.1016/j.bdr.2015.04.001
6. Zareiforoush, H., Minaei, S., Alizadeh, M.R., Banakar, A.: Potential applications of computer vision in quality inspection of rice: a review. Food Eng. Rev. **7**(3), 321–345 (2015). http://dx.doi.org/10.1007/s12393-014-9101-z
7. Grinberg, N.F., Orhobor, O.I., King, R.D.: An evaluation of machine-learning for predicting phenotype: studies in yeast, rice, and wheat. Mach. Learn. **109**(2), 251–277 (2019). http://dx.doi.org/10.1007/s10994-019-05848-5
8. Lin, P., Li, X.L., Chen, Y.M., He, Y.: A deep convolutional neural network architecture for boosting image discrimination accuracy of rice species. Food Bioprocess Technol. **11**(4), 765–773 (2018). https://doi.org/10.1007/s11947-017-2050-9
9. Liu, T., et al.: A shadow-based method to calculate the percentage of filled rice grains. Biosyst. Eng. **150**, 79–88 (2016). http://dx.doi.org/10.1016/j.biosystemseng.2016.07.011
10. Ahmed, T., Rahman, C.R., Abid, M.F.M.: Rice grain disease identification using dual phase convolutional neural network based system aimed at small dataset (2020). https://arxiv.org/abs/2004.09870
11. Cinar, I., Koklu, M.: Classification of rice varieties using artificial intelligence methods. Int. J. Intell. Syst. Appl. Eng. **7**(3), 188–194 (2019). http://dx.doi.org/10.18201/ijisae.2019355381
12. Naik, H.S., et al.: A real-time phenotyping framework using machine learning for plant stress severity rating in soybean. Plant Methods **13**(1) (2017). http://dx.doi.org/10.1186/s13007-017-0173-7
13. Ebrahimi, E., Mollazade, K., Babaei, S.: Toward an automatic wheat purity measuring device: a machine vision-based neural networks-assisted imperialist competitive algorithm approach. Measurement **55**, 196–205 (2014). http://dx.doi.org/10.1016/j.measurement.2014.05.003
14. Liu, T., Chen, W., Wu, W., Sun, C., Guo, W., Zhu, X.: Detection of aphids in wheat fields using a computer vision technique. Biosyst. Eng. **141**, 82–93 (2016). https://doi.org/10.1016/j.biosystemseng.2015.11.005
15. Olgun, M., et al.: Wheat grain classification by using dense sift features with SVM classifier. Comput. Electron. Agri. **122**, 185–190 (2016). https://doi.org/10.1016/j.compag.2016.01.033
16. Koklu, M., Ozkan, I.A.: Multiclass classification of dry beans using computer vision and machine learning techniques. Comput. Electron. Agri. **174**, 105507 (2020). http://dx.doi.org/10.1016/j.compag.2020.105507
17. Kaya, E., Saritas, I.: Towards a real-time sorting system: Identification of vitreous durum wheat kernels using ANN based on their morphological, colour, wavelet and gaborlet features. Comput. Electron. Agri. **166**, 105016 (2019). http://dx.doi.org/10.1016/j.compag.2019.105016
18. Han, L., Haleem, M.S., Taylor, M.: A novel computer vision-based approach to automatic detection and severity assessment of crop diseases. In: 2015 Science and Information Conference (SAI). IEEE (2015). https://doi.org/10.1109/SAI.2015.7237209
19. Shrestha, B.L., Kang, Y.M., Yu, D., Baik, O.D.: A two-camera machine vision approach to separating and identifying laboratory sprouted wheat kernels. Biosyst. Eng. **147**, 265–273 (2016). http://dx.doi.org/10.1016/j.biosystemseng.2016.04.008

20. Sabanci, K., Kayabasi, A., Toktas, A.: Computer vision-based method for classification of wheat grains using artificial neural network. J. Sci. Food Agri. **97**(8), 2588–2593 (2016). http://dx.doi.org/10.1002/jsfa.8080
21. Pires, R.D.L., et al.: Local descriptors for soybean disease recognition. Comput. Electron. Agri. **125**, 48–55 (2016). http://dx.doi.org/10.1016/j.compag.2016.04.032

Managing and Controlling IP Packet Traffic Based on AI at Router on Internet: A Survey

Vuong Xuan Chi[(⊠)], Nguyen Kim Quoc, and Phan Thi Tuoi

Faculty of Information Technology, Nguyen Tat Thanh University, Ho Chi Minh City, Vietnam
{vxchi,nkquoc,pttuoi}@ntt.edu.vn

Abstract. Today, the increasing volume of data and the rising demand for user-requested information exchange necessitate ensuring optimal performance for internet communication networks, especially within complex systems. Additionally, most real-time applications require high-speed data transmission, creating uneven traffic flows that lead to local congestion and impact the quality of service (QoS). To maintain a sustainable and high-performance network, it is crucial to implement mechanisms to prevent network packet congestion. In this study, we survey recent scientific research that uses artificial intelligence (AI) to control traffic at routers, identifying future challenges to address congestion issues, particularly in managing and controlling network traffic to ensure network performance at internet routers.

Keywords: ip packet · network congestion · traffic control · routers · network performance

1 Introduction

The paper provides an overview and detailed analysis of issues and solutions related to congestion in IP networks at routers, along with traffic control mechanisms that help deepen the understanding of this field. It also outlines future research directions and challenges in optimizing AI-based traffic control methods for congestion management at routers.

Many traffic control techniques, performance optimization, and network security methods leverage various machine learning (ML) approaches, focusing on clustering, classification, regression, and reinforcement learning (RL). Research contributes to and compares congestion control methods that apply AI techniques, such as ML problems [4, 12], but there are also more specific challenges. Additionally, the comparison of supervised ML models applied to IP packet classification using techniques like Logistic Regression (LR), Support Vector Machine (SVM), Random Forest (RF), Linear Discriminant Analysis (LDA), K-Neighbors Classifier (KNN), Naive Bayes Gaussian (GNB), and Decision Tree (DT) [17] also faces limitations due to the research being conducted in data centers. A review of network traffic classification techniques and ML-based methods for traffic classification [18] highlights research challenges and identifies several

P. Cong Vinh et al. (Eds.): ICTCC 2024, LNICST 668, pp. 27–56, 2026.
https://doi.org/10.1007/978-3-032-12846-1_3

recommendations and suggestions for future research directions in traffic classification. Additionally, a survey provides a discussion on future directions and open research issues, particularly focusing on packet classi-fication using unsupervised learning algorithms. These algorithms include K-means clustering, hierarchical clustering, anomaly detection, principal component analysis, Apriori algorithm, Gaussian Mixture Models, and Manifold learning. This highlights the trend of using unsupervised ML in complex network data to improve network performance and service delivery, classify Internet traffic, manage traffic, detect anomalies, and optimize QoS [42, 63]. Additionally, Neural Network (NN) and Deep Learning (DL) algorithms have been extensively researched in TCP papers to estimate congestion control algorithms using Deep Recurrent Neural Network (DRNN) based classification [36]. Despite demonstrating great potential to improve network performance, it remains a significant challenge to apply AI-based algorithms in real-world network environments due to the increasing complexity of current network architectures and protocols.

In this paper, the remaining sections are organized as follows. Section 2 covers related research. Specifically, Sect. 2.1 presents several related studies on mechanisms and algorithms for traffic control and congestion management using AI technology in TCP protocols and queues. In Sect. 2.2, we describe the architecture of network routers and related operations. Section 2.3 investigates the structure of the IP header in IP packets. Section 2.4 introduces research subjects through a diagram related to traffic control improvements and congestion management at routers.

Next, in Sect. 3, Sect. 3.1 discusses supervised and unsupervised learning algorithms, compares these two types of machine learning, and analyzes congestion management and traffic control through AI technology, such as IP packet classification using ML to ensure QoS. Section 3.2 addresses the causes of congestion and AI- based TCP congestion control mechanisms. Section 3.3 describes active queue management (AQM) mechanisms and algorithms that apply ML and DL. Section 3.4 covers Software defined networks (SDN) using AI to make networks more flexible, ena-bling cloud and network administrators to quickly respond to changing demands through a centralized controller. Section 4, the article provides research results such as advantages and disadvantages of related studies, evaluates research results and presents new research challenges in the future. Finally, Sect. 5, concludes the paper, summarizing the survey results and the challenge of managing congestion through traffic control at AI-based IP network routers.

2   Related Works

2.1   Mechanisms and Algorithms Using AI Technology for Congestion Management in Networks.

TCP control mechanisms such as TCP Tahoe, TCP Reno, TCP Vegas, TCP SACK, FAST TCP, TCP Westwood in [5, 6, 8] provide advantages and drawbacks, yet they pose significant challenges in managing network congestion at routers. Research related to monitoring packet delay to enhance performance also explores networks capable of handling complexities like delay and disruption tolerance (DTN), which have been shown to exhibit varying effectiveness in different situations and conditions [7]. Research has also investigated adapting an easily usable theoretical optimization model for TCP-Gentle, demonstrating its capability to compete with existing TCP variants.

However, challenges remain in validating the algorithm across different network link structures, such as issues arising from bidirectional network traffic under varying conditions [9]. The Transmission Control Protocol (TCP) focuses on four functions (slow start, congestion avoidance algorithm, fast retransmit, and fast recovery) applied to control congestion impact differently across connection links from PPP DS1 to PPP DS3 concerning network performance, albeit insignificantly [10]. Additionally, the TCP/IP congestion control mechanism increasingly struggles to respond effectively to the most common behavior of Internet traffic, severely impacting performance and failing to guarantee service quality [11, 13].

Congestion is a primary issue caused by excessive traffic in the network beyond its capacity. Models utilize intelligent algorithms to understand congestion capabilities at routers [35], applying ML to address network congestion issues at routers. Experiments focus on parameters such as sliding window (CWND), throughput, RTT, packet loss rate, and fairness.

Moreover, traditional models combined with modern adaptations demonstrate the ability to adapt and achieve high performance consistently across diverse network conditions for congestion control [37]. Network traffic classification, enabling quality of service monitoring and efficient bandwidth management [19], primarily addresses the load balancing issue. DL and RL techniques [38] pose significant challenges when applying congestion control based on RL in the real world, including fairness and network security. In practical scenarios, RL-based congestion algorithms are affected by the computation time required for RL [15]. The Deep Q-Network (DQN) algorithm implements the TCP-DQN method and compares it with major congestion control algorithms. The results show that TCP-DQN's throughput can be more than twice that of conventional methods [14]. Additionally, DQN focuses on reinforcing deep learning in managing latency and balancing between queue delay and throughput, comparing it to the better performance results of Random Early Detection (RED) by more than 2% margin [32].

Artificial Neural Networks (ANN) [1, 2], Genetic Algorithms (GA), AQM mechanisms at routers [3, 26, 27]. Mechanisms and algorithms related to active queue management such as RED, Flow Random Early Drop (FRED), Adaptive Random Early Detection (ARED), CHOose and Kill for unresponsive flows, CHOose and Keep for responsive flows (CHOKe), Bottleneck Link Utilization Estimator (BLUE), Stochastic Fair BLUE (SFB), Rate Adaptive Queueing (RaQ) [20], the authors of this work identify shortcomings and compare the performance of these algorithms, while also proposing directions for extending new algorithms to achieve better benefits. In particular, the RED mechanism has been enhanced to monitor latency at routers and perform packet discarding to address network delay issues and enhance network performance [22, 23, 30]. The Quadratic Early Random Early Detection (QERED) algorithm aims to improve the performance of the RED algorithm [34]. The integrated IRED method proposed outperforms state-of-the-art approaches in packet loss and delay reduction, achieving respective reduction rates of 18% and 10.6% [31]. The DyRED algorithm is an advanced congestion control algorithm [25].

Fuzzy logic (FL) systems [16, 21] propose adaptive fuzzy control methods with specified constraints to ensure real-time state and stable performance of error monitoring can be met. Additionally, the Grey Wolf Optimizer (GWO) algorithm is used in designing a proportional integral fuzzy system (fuzzy-PI) as a new AQM for internet congestion control at routers, aiming to achieve stability and quick response while reducing errors [24]. Furthermore, the Adaptive Neuro-Fuzzy Inference System (ANFIS) acts like a PID controller for AQM. This model utilizes genetic algorithms (GA) and particle swarm optimization (PSO) to optimize all variables [28, 33], surpassing in stability, convergence, recovery capability, loss rate reduction, and minimizing data transfer delays in network congestion [29].

In addition, several studies present monitoring systems that are accurate, user-friendly, and sufficiently fast to reflect network performance in real-time. These systems consider factors such as latency, bandwidth, throughput, packet loss rate, application prioritization, and user experience [40]. Thus, evaluating performance and Quality of Service (QoS), determining the network's responsiveness to specific requirements, helps ascertain if the network meets QoS requirements and assesses the impact of congestion on service quality [46].

In this study, we describe the structure and operation mechanisms of the network router. Additionally, we introduce the structure of the IP header, which comprises 12 fundamental attributes. Following this, we provide an overview diagram of AI model approaches for network traffic management and congestion control at the router.

2.2 Network Router Architecture

According to the architecture of a network router, it consists of three layers: classification, queue, and scheduler as depicted in Fig. 1.

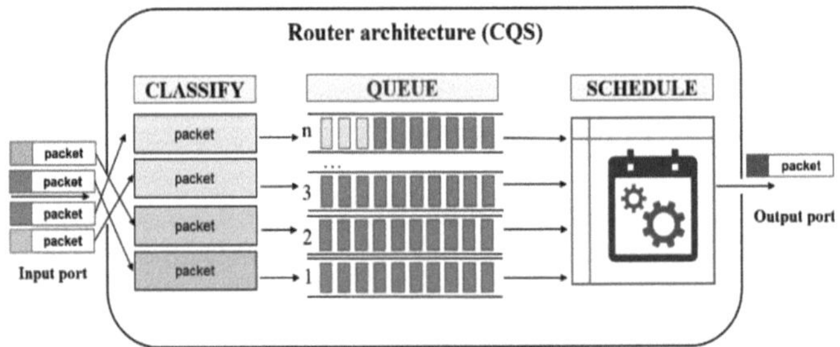

Fig. 1. Network Router Architecture

When packets enter the network router, they are first classified based on their header fields to distinguish their functions. The network assigns priority levels to these packets, which are used to manage network congestion. Next, packets are queued to ensure traffic flow, especially at bottleneck routers. The principle is to enqueue packets if the queue is not full, drop packets if the queue is full, and dequeue packets when requested by the scheduler. At the third layer, scheduling ensures that packets from multiple queues exit through the same interface without contention, thereby avoiding output congestion.

2.3 IP Header of a Packet

Packet data consists of information that is segmented and encapsulated within packets for transmission across networks. These packets contain details such as source and destination addresses, network protocols, IP addresses, technical parameters of the transmission path, actual data to be transmitted, and other relevant information. The IP packet structure is used in various network protocols to transmit packets across the internet. The IP packet structure comprises a header and data. The specific fields of the IP header include 12 mandatory attributes, totaling 20 bytes in length (excluding Data and Options). Refer to Table 1 for a description of the IPv4 Header structure.

Table 1. Structure of IP Header (Version 4)

Version	IHL	Type of Service	Total Length	
Identification			Flags	Fragment Offset
Time to Live		Protocol	Header Checksum	
Source IP Address				
Destination IP Address				
IP Options			Padding	
Data				

In which: Version is the version of the IP protocol, usually IPv4 or IPv6; Internet Header Length (IHL): length of IP header, unit is 32bit words, minimum value of IHL is 5 and maximum is 15; Type of Service (TOS): information of requested service and packet priority service; Total Length: total IP packet size, in bytes; Identification: used to identify related packets during packet fragmentation and reassembly; Flags: The first 3 bits of a 16bit field, used to determine whether a packet has been fragmented or not, or is the last packet in the fragmentation process; Fragment Offset: position of each fragment in the packet after fragmentation; Time to Live (TTL): is the time to exist (live) of an IP packet, calculated in seconds. When it passes through a router, the TTL value is reduced by one unit; Protocol: used to encapsulate data in packets; Header Checksum: integrity of the IP header; Source Address: determines the source IP address of the packet; Destination Address: determines the destination IP address of the packet and Options: an optional field, which may or may not be in the IP header, used for purposes such as measuring latency and measuring quality of service in IP networks [39].

2.4 Scope and Objects of Study

In this study, we provide a comprehensive survey and analysis of recent scientific works focusing on network service quality, IP packet classification criteria using ML, and IP network QoS assessment through latency, bandwidth, and packet loss rate evaluation [18, 41].

We examine algorithms and protocols leveraging AI technology for TCP congestion control, AQM mechanisms using AI, and SDN-enabled networks using AI. Through our survey targets, we can outline the strengths and weaknesses of existing research efforts,

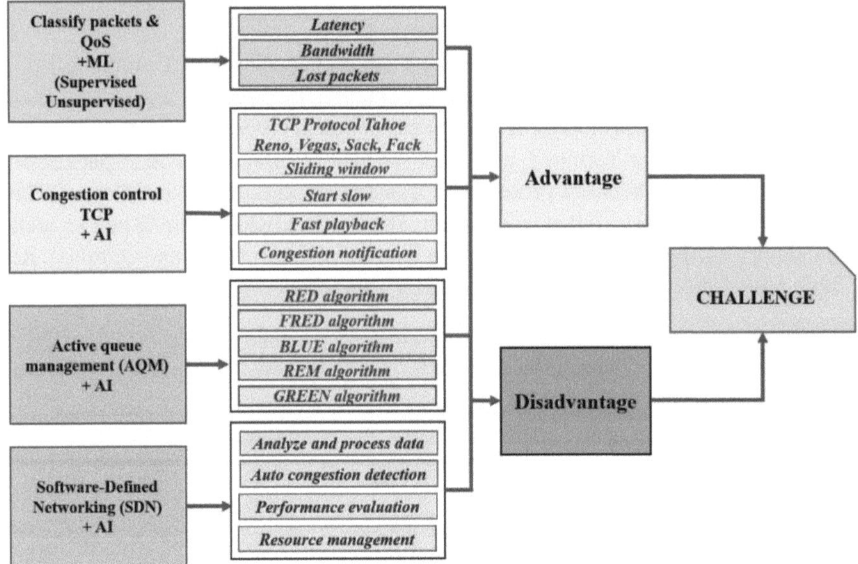

Fig. 2. The survey diagram outlines the overall factors influencing network congestion

identifying unresolved issues and research challenges in managing and controlling IP network traffic at routers on the internet. See research survey overview in Fig. 2.

3 Approach AI Technology to Manage and Control Network Traffic

3.1 Classify IP Packets Using ML, Ensuring QoS

Classifying IP network traffic is a very important task because it allows for better management and planning [41]. Here, we compare ML algorithms, including supervised learning algorithms as follows:

- **Support Vector Machine (SVM)**

SVM is a supervised ML algorithm used for classification and regression. It seeks a hyperplane in the highest dimensional feature space to separate data into two different classes with the maximum possible margin between them. This hyperplane maximizes the margin of safety between the classes.

SVM finds a hyperplane $\mathbf{w}\mathbf{x} + \mathbf{b} = 0$ to separate data classes with the maximum margin. The optimization formula for SVM is:

$$\min_{\mathbf{w},b} \frac{1}{2} \|\mathbf{w}\|^2 \text{ subject to } y_i(\mathbf{w} \cdot \mathbf{x}_i + b) \geq 1, \forall i \tag{1}$$

- **Logistic Regression (LR)**

Logistic Regression (LR) is a statistical method to predict the probability of a binary variable based on independent variables. This algorithm uses a sigmoid function to map any real-valued input to the range (0, 1), and then applies a threshold for classification. LR utilizes the sigmoid function to predict class probabilities. The sigmoid function is defined as:

$$\sigma(z) = \frac{1}{1 + e^{-z}} \tag{2}$$

The function that predicts the class probability is:

$$P(y = 1|x) = \sigma(\mathrm{w} \cdot \mathrm{x} + b) \tag{3}$$

The loss function is log-loss:

$$\mathcal{L} = -\frac{1}{\mathbf{N}} \sum_{\mathbf{i}=1}^{\mathbf{N}} \left[\mathbf{y_i} \mathbf{log}(\hat{y}_{\mathbf{i}}) + (1 - \mathbf{y_i}) \mathbf{log}(1 - \hat{y}_{\mathbf{i}}) \right] \tag{4}$$

- **Random Forest Classifier**

Random Forest is an ensemble of many decision trees built on random samples of the data. Each tree in the forest votes for its class, and the final class is chosen by majority vote. Each decision tree T_m predicts the class $\hat{y}_m$. The final prediction is the average or mode of predictions from all the trees:

$$\hat{y} = \mathrm{mode}(\{\hat{y}_1, \hat{y}_2, \ldots, \hat{y}_M\}) \tag{5}$$

- **K-Neighbors Classifier (KNN)**

KNN is a classification algorithm based on distance. A new data point is classified based on the labels of the k nearest neighbors in the feature space. Distance is typically measured using Euclidean distance.

$$\hat{y} = \mathrm{mode}\left(\left\{y_{i_1}, y_{i_2}, \ldots, y_{i_k}\right\}\right) \tag{6}$$

- **Naive Bayes Gaussian (Gaussian NB)**

Naive Bayes is a group of algorithms based on Bayes' theorem with the strong assumption that features are independent of each other. Gaussian Naive Bayes assumes that features follow a Gaussian (normal) distribution.

$$\mathbf{P(y|x)} \propto \mathbf{P(y)} \prod_{\mathbf{i}=1}^{\mathbf{n}} \mathbf{P(x_i|y)} \tag{7}$$

where $P(x_i \mid y)$ is Gaussian distribution:

$$P(x_i|y) = \frac{1}{\sqrt{2\pi\sigma_y^2}} \exp\left(-\frac{(x_i - \mu_y)^2}{2\sigma_y^2}\right) \tag{8}$$

- **Linear Discriminant Analysis (LDA)**

LDA finds optimal linear separators by maximizing the distance between classes and minimizing within-class variation.

$$\delta_k(\mathrm{x}) = \mathrm{x}^T \Sigma^{-1} \mu_k - \frac{1}{2}\mu_k^T \Sigma^{-1} \mu_k + \log P(y = k) \tag{9}$$

- **Decision Tree Classifier (DT)**

Decision Tree (DT) is a prediction model that uses a tree structure to determine the target value of a variable by learning simple decision rules from input features. Each node in the tree represents a condition on a feature, and each branch represents the outcome of that condition. DT uses split points to partition the data. Common branching criteria include entropy and Gini index.

$$H(S) = -\sum_{i=1}^{C} p_i \log_2 p_i \tag{10}$$

where p_i is the probability of class i in the node.

Gini index is:

$$G(S) = 1 - \sum_{i=1}^{C} p_i^2 \tag{11}$$

The decision tree will choose the optimal split point to minimize the entropy or Gini index.

There is several machine learning algorithms used for IP packet classification, each having its advantages and disadvantages [45]. This paper comprehensively evaluates network traffic classification methods from five perspectives: statistical based classification, correlation-based classification, behavior-based classification, payload-based classification, and port-based classification. Choosing the right traffic classification algorithm plays a crucial role in achieving proper and effective traffic classification. Various machine learning methods are widely used in network traffic classification. Article [49] addresses a method to meet real-time requirements for network traffic classification while ensuring user privacy protection. By anonymizing IP addresses and using a 12byte IP packet header, the proposed model achieves high accuracy and low time complexity, as demonstrated in experiments on three open-source datasets.

The shortcomings of the machine learning algorithm in Table 2 show many challenges that need to be resolved for effective application in the problems of classifying and predicting IP packet traffic at routers. IP packet classification requires storing and processing large amounts of network data. Make sure the system has enough memory resources or use memory optimization techniques such as data compression and efficient memory management. When dealing with imbalanced data, techniques like oversampling, undersampling, or adjusting weights improve performance. Simultaneously, optimizing algorithms and using powerful hardware such as GPUs reduce computational costs. In networks, packet attributes often correlate with each other. Therefore, it is essential to use models capable of handling attribute dependencies, such as graph-based models or more complex models like deep neural networks. Understanding these

Table 2. Advantages and disadvantages of classification algorithms

Algorithms	Advantages	Disadvantages
Support Vector Machine (SVM)	Improves generalization performance, can solve high-dimensional and nonlinear problems	High memory costs
Logistic Regression	Fast training, dynamic adjustment of classification thresholds	Easy to over-adjust, handle complex features
Random Forest Classifier	Not easy to overfit, quick training	Not suitable for small and low-dimensional data sets
K-Neighbors Classifier (KNN)	Simple, does not assume characteristics, suitable for diverse classification problems	Poor performance on imbalanced data sets, high computational cost.
Naive Bayes Gaussian (Gaussian NB)	High accuracy, fewer estimated parameters, and insensitivity to extraneous data	The assumption that required properties are mutually independent is difficult to satisfy
Decision Tree Classifier	Small calculation volume, fast classification	Suitable for high-dimensional data; prone to overfitting, ignoring correlations between data features

drawbacks helps design and implement more effective IP packet classification systems on the internet. This remains a challenge when applying AI techniques to classification problems. Specifically:

– Optimize memory and computational resources.
– Use techniques to reduce overfitting and handle imbalanced data.
– Select models that fit the characteristics and size of the IP packet data.
– Consider the relationships between attributes to improve model accuracy.

Additionally, measuring queue delay presents a challenge as it requires substantial infrastructure support for testing. To measure queue delay on a router using the probe gap model, the paper employs a common data clustering algorithm to process its data samples. This approach ensures that measurement effectiveness is not hindered by infrastructure access issues, variations in probe gaps, or the number of clusters in data processing. To measure queue delay on a single path, including a router connecting source and destination network nodes, the proposed method in the study proves effective [47, 48] is as follows:

First, the router sends a sequence of n packet pairs, each pair consisting of a small packet P_h and a large packet P_t with no separation in between, from source to destination. Details about the sizes of P_h and P_h on a one-hop path are available.

- Timestamp P_h and P_t each packet pair travels from src to dst, and the measurement involves determining n gaps between probes at the destination.
- Processing the measured gaps uses the k-means clustering algorithm to divide them into three different clusters.
- Label the clusters as *co*, *nc* and *de* for compression, no change, and decompression, respectively, in the packet pairs so that the cluster centroids (M_{co}, M_{nc} và M_{de}) have the following relationship:

$$M_{co} < M_{nc} < M_{de} \tag{12}$$

- Determine the queue delay on the router from the centroid:

  • Calculate queuing delay (w_{co}) from compression:

$$w_{co} = M_{nc} - M_{co} \tag{13}$$

  • Estimate queuing delay (w_{de}) from decompression:

$$w_{de} = M_{de} - M_{nc} \tag{14}$$

  • Estimate overall queuing delay (w):

$$w = \sum_{i=\{co,de\}} w_i \bar{s}_i \tag{15}$$

  where $\bar{s}_i$ is the weighted cluster size, e.g., $\bar{s}_{co} = \frac{s_{co}}{s_{co}+s_{de}}$.
  • Estimate the variability (σ) in w:

$$\sigma = \sqrt{\frac{1}{n'-1}\sum_{j=1}^{n'}\left(x_j - w\right)^2} \tag{16}$$

  where $x_j \in \{co, de\}$ and $n\prime = s_{co} + s_{de}$.

Report a range of queuing delays estimated over the single-hop path as $w \pm \sigma$.

Besides supervised machine learning technology, classification also applies unsupervised learning [42, 64]. Unsupervised machine learning algorithms include:

- **K-means clustering**

K-means is a simple and popular clustering algorithm. Its goal is to partition data into K clusters such that points within the same cluster are similar to each other and different from points in other clusters. The K-means algorithm minimizes the sum of squared distances between data points and their cluster centroids.

$$\min\sum_{i=1}^{K}\sum_{\mathbf{x}\in C_i}\|\mathbf{x} - \mu_i\|^2 \tag{17}$$

where μ_i is the center of cluster C_i.

- **Hierarchical clustering (HC)**

Hierarchical clustering (HC) is a clustering algorithm that constructs a dendrogram showing the hierarchical order of clusters. There are two main methods: single linkage and complete linkage.

Single linkage: the distance between two clusters is the smallest distance between any pair of points in the two clusters.

$$d\left(C_i, C_j\right) = \min_{\mathbf{x} \in C_i, \mathbf{y} \in C_j} \|\mathbf{x} - \mathbf{y}\| \tag{18}$$

The distance between two clusters is the largest distance between any pair of points in the two clusters.

$$d\left(C_i, C_j\right) = \max_{\mathbf{x} \in C_i, \mathbf{y} \in C_f} \|\mathbf{x} - \mathbf{y}\| \tag{19}$$

- **Anomaly detection (DA)**

DA is the process of identifying data points that do not follow the expected pattern or trend in the data set. There are many methods of anomaly detection, including using Gaussian distributions or distance-based techniques.

Suppose a data point x is anomalous if its probability of following a Gaussian distribution is low:

$$p(\mathbf{x}) = \frac{1}{(2\pi)^{n/2}|\Sigma|^{1/2}} \exp\left(-\frac{1}{2}(\mathbf{x} - \mu)^T \Sigma^{-1}(\mathbf{x} - \mu)\right) \tag{20}$$

where μ and Σ are the mean and covariance matrix.

- **Principal component analysis (PCA)**

PCA is a method of reducing data dimensionality by finding principal components such that these axes are orthogonal vectors that maximize the variance of the data. PCA finds the eigenvectors v and eigenvalues λ from the covariance matrix Σ: $\Sigma v = \lambda v$

- **Apriori Algorithm**

Apriori is an algorithm used in association rule mining. The algorithm finds frequent itemsets in transaction databases and generates association rules. Association rules have the form $A \rightarrow B$ with measures of confidence and lift.

$$\text{confidence } (A \rightarrow B) = \frac{\text{support}(A \cup B)}{\text{support}(A)} \tag{21}$$

$$\text{lift}(A \rightarrow B) = \frac{\text{support}(A \cup B)}{\text{support}(A) \cdot \text{support}(B)} \tag{22}$$

- **Gaussian Mixture Models (GMM)**

GMM is a probability model comprising multiple Gaussian distributions, with each distribution representing a cluster in the data. GMM uses the Expectation Maximization (EM) algorithm to find the parameters of the Gaussian distributions.

$$p(\mathbf{x}) = \sum_{k=1}^{K} \pi_k \mathcal{N}(\mathbf{x} \mid \mu_k, \Sigma_k) \tag{23}$$

where π_k is the weight of the Gaussian distribution $\mathcal{N}(\mathbf{x} \mid \mu_k, \Sigma_k)$.

- **Manifold Learning**

Manifold Learning is a group of machine learning techniques used to reduce the dimensionality of data in nonlinear spaces. Popular algorithms include t-SNE (t-Distributed Stochastic Neighbor Embedding) and ISOMAP (Isometric Mapping). t-SNE reduces data dimensionality by minimizing the difference between probability distributions in high-dimensional space and low dimensional space.

$$\mathrm{KL}(P\|Q) = \sum_{i \neq j} P_{ij} \log \frac{P_{ij}}{Q_{ij}} \tag{24}$$

where P_{ij} and Q_{ij} are the probabilities of point pairs in high and low dimensional space.

From the article [64] [67–69], unsupervised machine learning algorithms give advantages and disadvantages as shown in Table 3.

Machine learning, both supervised and unsupervised, are data driven methods but differ in how they utilize data and their ultimate objectives. Supervised learning relies on labeled data to predict specific outcomes, whereas unsupervised learning seeks patterns and hidden structures within unlabeled data. Both have wide ranging applications and are crucial in various fields. Table 4 outlines the differences between supervised and unsupervised learning types.

Table 4. Compare the difference between supervised and unsupervised learning.

Implementation	Supervised learning	Unsupervised learning
Training data	Need labeled data.	No need for labeled data.
Purpose	Predict results or classify new data points based on known labels.	Explore data structure, looking for patterns or relationships in data.
Performance evaluation	Performance is often evaluated based on metrics such as accuracy, sensitivity, and specificity.	Performance is often more difficult to evaluate due to the lack of labels.
Popular algorithm	Linear Regression, Logistic Regression, Decision Trees, Random Forests, SVM, Neural Networks.	K-means Clustering, Hierarchical Clustering, DBSCAN, PCA, t-SNE, Apriori, Gaussian Mixture Models.

3.2 TCP Anti-congestion Protocol Combines AI Technology

Congestion is a common phenomenon on networks, characterized by rapidly increasing packet delays, packet loss rates, and a sharp decrease in throughput. The Internet operates on a store and forward principle, where incoming packets are stored in queues at routers, awaiting processing to be forwarded along a selected path to their destination. As the volume of incoming packets grows, network congestion prolongs processing times,

Table 3. The advantages and disadvantages of unsupervised machine learning algorithms

Algorithm / No. Ref	Advantages	Disadvantages
K-means clustering [67, 69]	The large number of variables, K-means will be faster than hierarchical clustering. When recomputing the centroid, the cluster of an instance may be modified.	The number of groups in the network (k value) and other initial inputs are strongly influenced by the output. The number of clusters or the value of k cannot be determined.
Hierarchical clustering [69]	Easy to understand, no need for preset clusters, flexible, creates natural hierarchy.	Computationally expensive, poor scalability, unable to reconstruct divisions, sensitive to noise.
Anomaly detection [67, 69]	Detects anomalies flexibly across various data types, requires less anomaly data, enhances security and monitoring.	Difficult to determine thresholds, high false positive rates, depends on data quality, struggles with dynamic data.
Principal component analysis [64, 69]	Based on linear algebra that computers can quickly solve. Regression easily adapts to handling multidimensional data issues.	Principal components have low interpretability. No distinction between dimension reduction and information loss.
Apriori [64, 69]	On large datasets, the algorithm's pruning and merging stages are straightforward.	Predecessor algorithms have particularly high complexity in both space and time.
Gaussian Mixture Models [68, 69]	Flexible, probabilistic distribution, handles missing data, automatically determines cluster number.	Depends on normal distribution, local optimization, sensitive to initialization, computationally expensive.
Manifold Learning [69]	Efficient data dimensionality reduction, preserves local structure, widely applicable, handles nonlinear data processing.	Complex and costly, challenging in interpretation, sensitive to parameters, not applicable to all data types.

increases the number of discarded packets due to queue overflow, and poses the risk of complete network paralysis.

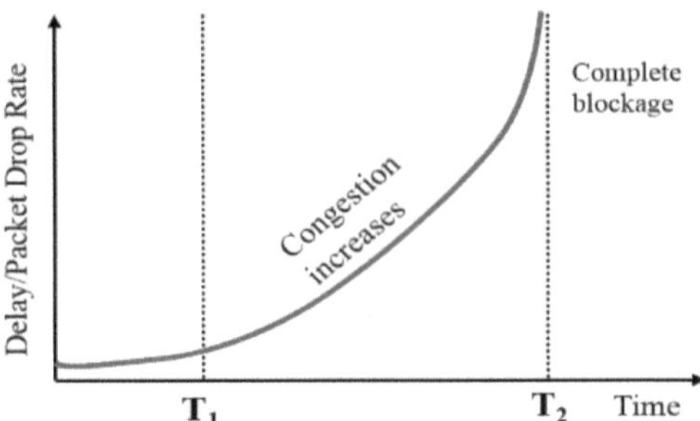

a. The relationship between the variables over time.

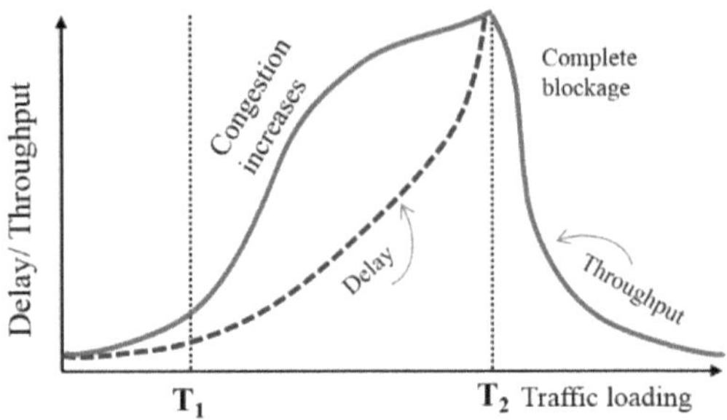

b. The relationship between the variables over the traffic load.

Fig. 3. Network congestion evolution over time and under increasing traffic load

Figure 3 a depicts congestion scenarios with delay and packet loss rate over time. Figure 3b illustrates the relationship between delay, and throughput corresponding to traffic load (number of packets sent into the network). Congestion occurs within the interval [T1, T2] where delay and packet loss rate increase rapidly with traffic load. At time T2, the network is nearly congested completely, and delay and packet loss rates become very high. When fully congested, all packets are dropped. Congestion occurs due to several reasons, primarily:

- The sender's transmission rate exceeds the network link bandwidth end-to-end;
- Temporary packet storage queues for forwarding at intermediate routers become overloaded, leading to buffer overflow;
- Network routers (including both intermediate and destination routers) are unable to process incoming packets in time.

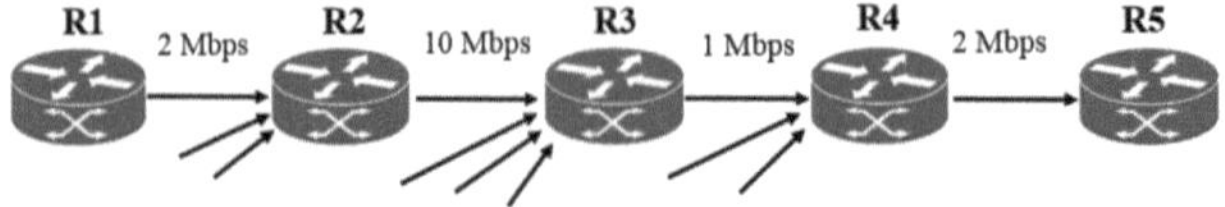

Fig. 4. Describe a simple case with 4 link segments.

The connection between routers R1-R2 and R4-R5 is through WiFi links with a bandwidth of 2 Mbps each, while the R2-R3 segment has a bandwidth of 10 Mbps, and the R3-R4 segment has a bandwidth of 1 Mbps (as it may be shared among multiple connections). The R3-R4 segment is referred to as the bottleneck bandwidth. The sender can only transmit at a speed of 1 Mbps, matching the bottleneck bandwidth. If the sender transmits over 1 Mbps, congestion will occur. The bottleneck bandwidth can occur at any segment depending on traffic variations. Its location fluctuates, making it challenging to determine because the number of connections changes randomly over time. R1, R2, R3, R4, R5 have bandwidths of 2 Mbps, 10 Mbps, 1 Mbps, 2 Mbps respectively. Figure 4 depicts a bottleneck congestion scenario.

To address this congestion, TCP congestion control algorithms leveraging AI technology are emerging, significantly mitigating congestion issues [12]. Current traffic management to prevent network congestion at routers combines traditional congestion control algorithms with AI, a field of extensive research facing numerous future challenges. The use of Reinforcement Learning (TCP-RL) techniques in TCP congestion control dynamically configures Initial Window (IW) and CWND to enhance TCP stream transmission performance [50]. In their paper [51], the authors apply RL and Deep Reinforcement Learning (DRL). RL learns congestion control policies optimally based on its observations of the network environment and past experiences, without relying on predefined rules, demonstrating strong adaptability to environmental changes. DRL harnesses the strengths of Deep Neural Networks in training processes, achieving scalability and improving learning speed.

In article [52], the authors present an experience-based method developed using a flexible Recurrent Neural Network (RNN), specifically LSTM networks, along with Deep Reinforcement Learning (DRL) to learn representations for all operational streams. Article [53] proposes the Eagle model, leveraging expert knowledge and employing DRL to train a generalized model aimed at learning from experts. The paper suggests improvements to transport layer protocols using various ML techniques on 5G networks; network monitoring using classification techniques like NN, DNN, and Random Forest (RF) algorithms could be beneficial for categorizing network activities across regions with sufficient training parameter sets, particularly employing RL techniques [65]. Fine tuning TCP CUBIC parameters to enhance congestion control, adjusting TCP Beta parameters of CUBIC, can improve congestion control capabilities using ML [66].

In Table 5, we survey and present the advantages and disadvantages of TCP congestion control approaches using ML and RL technologies, NN, DL [12, 50–53, 65, 66].

Table 5. Pros and Cons of TCP Congestion Control Algorithms with AI

Authors/Year/No. Ref	Tech.	Disadvantages	Advantages
Kong, Yiming, Hui Zang, and Xiaoli Ma (2018). [12]	LP-TCP, RL-TCP	Impact on the competitiveness of RL-TCP via NewReno.	TCP based on NewReno and Q-learning, LP-TCP and RL-TCP achieve better balance.

(continued)

Table 5. (*continued*)

Authors/Year/No. Ref	Tech.	Disadvantages	Advantages
Nie, Xiaohui, et al. (2019). [50]	TCP-RL	Results lack more detailed analysis and data on the effectiveness of TCP-RL compared to other methods.	Using RL to automatically configure appropriate IW (Initial Window) values.
Zhang, Ticao, and Shiwen Mao (2020). [51]	RL, DRL	Conventional TCP congestion control mechanisms based on predefined rules may not perform well in dynamic and complex networks.	RL-based schemes like QTCP, Aurora, and TCP-RL can autonomously configure congestion control parameters to adapt.
Xu, Zhiyuan, et al. (2019). [52].	RNN, LSTM, DRL	The performance of DRL-CC under complex network conditions has not been evaluated. Lack of stability and convergence analysis of DRL-CC.	The novel design of DRL-CC, integrating LSTM-based representation learning demonstrates the effectiveness and superiority of the DRL-based approach.
Emara, Salma, et al. (2020). [53]	DRL	Lack of evaluation on computational complexity and overhead of DRL-CC compared to traditional algorithms.	Learning from an expert helps the DRL agent start with a good policy rather than learning from scratch.
Poorzare, Reza, and Anna Calveras Augé (2020). [65]	RF	Focus on deploying TCP on 5G networks, but no mention of other transport protocols like QUIC or SCTP.	Analysis of TCP mechanisms, exploration of new approaches, and emphasizing the practical importance of the issue.
Knott, James (2023). [66]	TCP Beta, ML	Mainly focusing on optimizing the TCP CUBIC protocol without considering other transport protocols like QUIC, SCTP, or TCP variants.	The beta parameter in the TCP CUBIC algorithm plays a crucial role in influencing the protocol's response to network congestion.

3.3 Active Queue Management Mechanisms Apply ML and DL

In papers [30], the IM-RED and IRED algorithms develop from the inspiration of the simple design model of the RED model and implement the packet dropping function. They evaluate the performance of the proposed method compared to existing AQM methods such as RED, BLUE, ERED, FLRED, and EnRED using measures such as packet loss, packet drop, and delay. Additionally, the use of metrics displays network behavior during data transmission. The results in this study show that ARED performs better than RED, as presented in papers [56, 57]. The papers using Deep Q-network (DQN) and Fuzzy present simulation experiments that show the DQN and Fuzzy hybrid algorithms outperform the traditional RED algorithm in overall network performance. Additionally, to manage queues at network routers, there are several methods and algorithms with weaknesses in queue management. For example, the Droptail algorithm easily causes multiple packets drops in a single flow. AQM mechanisms like the RED and BLUE algorithms do not ensure fairness among flows. The Stochastic Fair Blue (SFB) algorithm does not use queue size information to mark packets. The Explicit Congestion Notification (ECN) method, the Fuzzy Explicit Window Adaptation (FEWA) method, and Core-Stateless Fair Queueing (CSFQ) face challenges in fully implementing congestion feedback methods at routers. Their scalability and applicability are limited, particularly in network segments where only a small portion of traffic flows through edge routers, making comprehensive deployment of these methods in IP network environments difficult to achieve. [59]. AQM algorithms include:

- **RED algorithm**

  RED is an active queue management algorithm used to prevent congestion in computer networks. RED mitigates congestion by randomly dropping packets when the queue length exceeds a certain threshold, providing early warning to data sources before the queue overflows. RED calculates the average queue length using a weighted exponential moving average filter. (Weighted Moving Average - WMA):

$$\text{avg\_queue\_length} = \left(1 - w_q\right) \times \text{avg\_queue\_length} + w_q \times \text{current\_queue\_length} \tag{25}$$

  In which, w_q is the smoothing coefficient.
  Compare the average queue length with the thresholds:

- If the average queue length is less than minth:
     Do not drop any packets.
- If the average queue length is between minth and maxth:
     Calculate the probability of dropping a packet.
- If the average queue length is greater than maxth:
     Drop all packets.

  Calculate the probability of dropping a packet.
  The probability of dropping a packet when the average queue length is between minth and maxth:

$$P = \frac{\text{avg\_queue\_length} - \text{minth}}{\text{maxth} - \text{minth}} \times \text{maxp} \tag{26}$$

When a packet is received, RED discards the packet with probability P.

In the paper [54], an improved mechanism FXRED uses the average queue length (avg) instead of the instantaneous queue length, continuously calculating the average queue length using a simple exponential weighted moving average. It then decides whether to accept or drop an incoming packet, comparing the calculated average value from the first stage with the average queue length threshold value.

- **FRED algorithm**

Flow Random Early Drop (FRED) is an AQM algorithm designed to enhance the performance of RED by considering individual traffic flows. FRED addresses several issues of RED, such as short-term flow bias and unfairness towards flows with low traffic.

FRED monitors individual traffic flows and adjusts its behavior based on these flows. Each traffic flow is independently tracked in terms of packet count in the queue.
FRED applies RED principles to each traffic flow separately, rather than applying them uniformly to all packets in the queue.
FRED aims to ensure that no single flow monopolizes resources by maintaining a minimum threshold for each flow.

When a flow exceeds this threshold, FRED increases the packet dropping probability for that flow to maintain fairness.

- **BLUE algorithm**

BLUE is an AQM algorithm designed to manage congestion in computer networks. Unlike algorithms like RED, BLUE does not rely on measuring the average queue length to determine when to drop packets. Instead, BLUE adjusts the packet dropping probability directly based on the packet loss rate and the queue waiting time.

Adjusting the packet dropping probability involves the following process and formula:

– *Increasing the packet dropping probability:*

When the queue is full or packets are lost, the packet dropping probability P_m is increased. Updates ensure that the packet dropping probability does not exceed 1.0.

$$P_m = \min(1.0, P_m + P_{inc}) \tag{27}$$

– *Reduce packet drop probability:*

When no packets are lost and the queue is not full, the packet dropping probability P_m is decreased. Updates ensure that the packet dropping probability does not decrease below 0.0.

$$P_m = \max(0.0, P_m - P_{dec}) \tag{28}$$

The packet dropping probability is updated only when the time since the last update exceeds P_{freeze}.
In which:

- P_m: The current packet dropping probability.
- P_{inc}: The packet dropping probability upon congestion detection.
- P_{dec}: The step by which the packet dropping probability decreases when congestion is not detected.
- P_{freeze}: The pause time between adjustments of the packet dropping probability.

- **SFB algorithm**

Stochastic Fair Blue (SFB) is a variant of the BLUE algorithm designed to provide a fair and efficient mechanism for network congestion control. SFB uses multiple virtual queues and hash functions to classify traffic streams into different queues, thereby adjusting packet dropping probabilities fairly.

- SFB employs multiple virtual queues to classify traffic streams.
- Each virtual queue maintains its own packet dropping probability state.
- Hash functions are used to assign packets to different virtual queues.
- This helps scatter packets randomly, reducing the likelihood of any one traffic stream monopolizing resources.
- SFB monitors packet loss rates and queueing delays in virtual queues to adjust packet dropping probabilities for each queue.

- *Increase packet dropping probability:*

When a virtual queue is full or packets are lost, the packet dropping probability $P_{m,i}$ for virtual queue i is increased. Update:

$$P_{m,i} = \min\left(1.0, P_{m,i} + P_{inc}\right) \tag{29}$$

- *Decrease packet dropping probability:*

When no packets are lost and the virtual queue is not full, the packet dropping probability $P_{m,i}$ for virtual queue i is decreased. Update:

$$P_{m,i} = \max\left(1.0, P_{m,i} - P_{dec}\right) \tag{30}$$

The superiority in performance of AQM anti-congestion mechanisms when applying AI is shown in Table 6, through evaluating the pros and cons of the mechanisms in articles [30, 31, 55–57, 60, 61].

Table 6. Advantages and disadvantages of studies at AQM

Authors/No. Ref	Year	Tech.	Disadvantages	Advantages

(continued)

Table 6. (*continued*)

Authors/No. Ref	Year	Tech.	Disadvantages	Advantages
Hassan, Samuel O., et al. [30]	2020	IM-RED	(IM-RED) innovatively addresses the shortcomings of the traditional RED algorithm by offering two elimination functions to manage congestion under varying network traffic load conditions	Limited application of AI techniques, improved algorithms are not outstanding compared to RED
Abu-Shareha, Ahmad Adel. [31]	2022	IRED	Better performance under various network conditions, especially under heavy and medium traffic.	Limited application of AI techniques, improved algorithms are not much compared to other algorithms
Yousif, Ayman Basheer; et al. [32]	2022	Deep Q-network (DQN)	Simulation experiments have shown that the DQN algorithm outperforms the traditional RED algorithm in terms of overall network performance.	Real-world applicability and potential biases in experimental design.
Hanan M. Kadhim, Ahmed A. Oglah [55]	2021	Fuzzy	The configured FPID (Fuzzy-PID) controller can perform congestion avoidance with good performance by monitoring the required reference queue size	Classic PID (Hybrid) controllers significantly improve congestion control on TCP/IP networks.

(*continued*)

Table 6. (*continued*)

Authors/No. Ref	Year	Tech.	Disadvantages	Advantages
Liu Zhengfei Jinsheng et al. [56]	2018	TCP	The model improves information compression entirely from the router by evaluating the average impact that an accepted/dropped packet has on the aggregate packet arrival rate.	AQM algorithms are required to be compatible with different network traffic scenarios.
Mustafa Maad Hamdi, et al. [57]	2021	TCP	The effectiveness of the Transmission Control Protocol (TCP) is significantly affected by Congestion Control.	The challenges and its effects on the performance of network communication have also been explained.
Ahmad F. AL-Allaf and A. I. A. Jabbar [58]	2019	OPNET	Reduces average queue size and queuing delay without affecting packet drop rate and link utilization.	Deploying the new AQM algorithm has not reduced costs.
Gilme'nez, Angel, et al. [60]	2022	BetaRED, ABetaRED, DBetaRED	The queue length remains stable with the parameters around a predetermined reference value when the network changes	Limit the use of AI techniques
Mahawish, Amar A., and Hassan J. [61]	2021	RED, FRED, WRED, GRED, DGREDCoDel AQM	Survey on different AQM algorithm schemes and their classification based on queue length, queue delay. Some algorithms may excel at achieving fairness between different streams	Many algorithms can be better at optimizing link utilization and link loss rates.

3.4 Software Defined Networks (SDN) Technique

SDN enhances traffic management at routers by separating control and forwarding, employing real-time analytics, and automating network control decisions. This improves network performance, reliability, and flexibility, better meeting the increasing demands of network applications and services.

- The SDN controller can apply traffic management policies to ensure Quality of Service (QoS) for various applications. For instance, critical traffic can be prioritized over non-critical traffic.
- The SDN controller can detect congestion points and adjust traffic to minimize impact.
- Measures such as traffic redirection or throttling can be applied.

Table 7 describes the main content ideas, frameworks, control methods, and the advantages and disadvantages of the algorithms applying SDN in [62].

Table 7. Advantages and disadvantages of algorithms using SDN

Algorithm	Main idea	Advantages	Disadvantages	Control	Control method
FTRS	Store the input stream and compress it with similar inputs	Reduce the number of stream inputs in the stream table	May not apply to some Internet applications	OpenDayLight	Cost, resource usage
FFTA	Flow table using FFTA and iFFTA techniques	Data Provides migration from existing networks to SDN	Inheriting the disadvantages of the BGP algorithm	PC system	Calculate a reasonable route
STAR	Delete expired stream entries, import new streams	Reduce workload and latency, while increasing average throughput	Not deployed on real platforms	PC system	Use stream table resources
Xu's method	Plan flows based on flow deadline constraints	Reduce energy consumption, increase efficiency and avoid expiration	Not tested on real platforms	OpenDayLight	Planning
Liu's method	Provides optimal thread update sequence	Reduce flow sheet requirements and improve update success rates	QoS and security policy are not guaranteed	Distributed controller	Set stream migration

(continued)

Table 7. (*continued*)

Algorithm	Main idea	Advantages	Disadvantages	Control	Control method
CeMon	Balance costs, flexibility, and manage operational flows	Reduce communication costs in different topologies	Synchronization problem of three algorithms	POX	Monitoring system
Afaq	Real-time detection and display of large flows	Redirect large flows to dedicated high-speed links	Lack of reviews in real platforms	FloodLight	Stream detection.

4   Research Results

Testing with collected access traffic data is conducted offline on the endpoint system, capturing frames using Wireshark at the University of Cordoba data center. The capturing process occurs during peak hours, specifically when there is high traffic demand. Within five hours timeframe, the data is stored in pcapng format, approximately 1.9 Gigabytes in size [6].

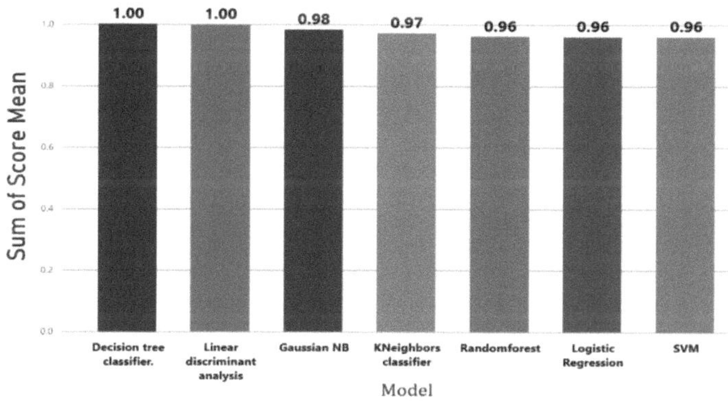

Fig. 5. The graph displays the average values across machine learning models

In Fig. 5, the mean score value of the Decision tree classifier model is the highest, but the differences are not significant. This indicates that no model currently outperforms others in classifying IP packets on the internet.

Machine learning algorithms with supervised learning are currently used to classify packets to ensure proper data stream service at routers. Through the survey, the paper identifies insights and research directions for future packet classification and network traffic management at routers using supervised ML algorithms, as shown in Table 8.

Table 8. Bottlenecks and challenges of supervised learning algorithms in packet classification

Algorithm	Current backlog	Future challenging trends
Support Vector Machine (SVM)	High memory costs.	Optimize memory costs and improve scalability.
Logistic Regression	Overfitting leads to poor performance with fluctuating real-world data.	Develop overfitting prevention techniques in dynamic network conditions.
Random Forest Classifier	Performance is unstable with small data and lack of dimensionality.	Optimize the algorithm for small and simple data.
K-Neighbors Classifier (KNN)	Poor performance with imbalanced data sets.	Develop methods to balance data and reduce computational costs.
Naive Bayes Gaussian (Gaussian NB)	Performance degrades when attributes are not independent.	Develop techniques to overcome the assumption of independence between attributes.
Decision Tree Classifier	Easy to overfit leading to poor performance in real-world situations.	Develop techniques to combat overfitting and improve generalization. Improve the ability to analyze and handle correlations between features.

Furthermore, by surveying unsupervised machine learning algorithms, we identify limitations and challenges for future applications in controlling packet traffic on the Internet, as depicted in Table 9. Applying unsupervised algorithms to IP packet classification and prediction can optimize and potentially enhance performance and accuracy in network analysis and monitoring.

Table 9. Backlog and challenges of unsupervised learning algorithms applied to packet classification

Algorithm	Current backlog	Developmental challenges
K-means Clustering	Rapid processing with large variable counts. Quickly change clusters when recalculating centroids.	Strongly depends on the number of clusters (k) and initial inputs. Ineffective with non-spherical cluster shapes.
Hierarchical Clustering	Easy to understand and no need to know the number of clusters beforehand. Provides flexibility and creates natural hierarchy.	Computationally expensive and does not scale well with large data. Cannot easily recover cluster divisions.

(continued)

Table 9. (continued)

Algorithm	Current backlog	Developmental challenges
Anomaly Detection	Requires minimal anomalous data for training. Enhances security and monitoring.	Difficult to determine accurate thresholds for anomaly detection. Depends on data quality and struggles with dynamic data.
Principal Component Analysis (PCA)	Rapid dimensionality reduction and easily executable on computers.	Principal components have low interpretability. Effective only with linear data.
Apriori Algorithm	Simplifies linkage stages and pruning on large datasets.	Very high complexity in space and time, challenging to apply in high-speed, high-volume network environments.
Gaussian Mixture Models (GMM)	Flexible and capable of handling missing data. Automatically determines the number of clusters.	Relies on the assumption of normal distribution. Prone to local optimization traps.
Manifold Learning	Efficient dimensionality reduction while preserving local structure. Widely applicable and processes nonlinear data effectively.	Complex and computationally expensive. Difficult to interpret results.

In addition, TCP congestion control algorithms, when combined with modern AI technology, highlight a number of opportunities and challenges through analyzing their advantages and disadvantages clearly shown in Table 10.

Table 10. Describe the opportunities and challenges of the TCP anti-congestion protocol combined with AI technology

Authors/Year/No. Ref	Tech.	Opportunity and challenge
Kong, Yiming, Hui Zang, and Xiaoli Ma (2018). [12]	LP-TCP, RL-TCP	The action space of RL-TCP may need to be redesigned depending on the network configuration. The information on integrating and deploying LP-TCP and RL-TCP solutions in real-world network systems.
Nie, Xiaohui, et al. (2019). [50]	TCP-RL	Information on integrating and deploying TCP-RL in real-world network systems.

(continued)

Table 10. (*continued*)

Authors/Year/No. Ref	Tech.	Opportunity and challenge
Zhang, Ticao, and Shiwen Mao (2020) [51]	RL, DRL	The need for real-world data collection, ensuring fairness and robustness while enabling multi-layer optimization.
Xu, Zhiyuan, et al. (2019). [52]	RNN, LSTM, DRL	The availability of computational resources and specialized ML libraries makes deploying congestion control based on DRL more feasible.
Emara, Salma, et al. (2020). [53]	DRL	Recent research has explored the use of offline learning techniques like Remy and Indigo, but they still have fixed mappings and are limited in the network environments they were trained on.
Poorzare Reza, and Anna Calveras Augé (2020). [65]	RF	TCP's inability to distinguish between packets lost due to congestion and those due to specific 5G network incidents could lead to throughput degradation.
Knott, James (2023). [66]	TCP Beta, ML	Besides Q-learning, exploring other ML algorithms such as DRL, Multi-Agent RL, or Federated Learning could be beneficial.

Moreover, the mechanisms and AQM algorithms also present bottlenecks and challenges when AI techniques are not applied, as shown in Table 11.

Table 11. Backlogs and challenges using AI to manage queues

Backlogs	Research challenges
– Not fully leveraging the power of AI in traffic management.	– Stronger integration with AI to enhance adaptability and performance.
– Actual performance may vary from simulated results.	– Enhance compatibility and optimization through AI.
– Limited application and complexity in configuration.	– Ensure the feasibility and effectiveness of DQN in real network environments.
– Difficulty in maintaining compatibility with diverse network conditions.	– Simplify configuration and increase adaptability of Fuzzy solutions.
– Performance may not be consistent across different network scenarios.	– Enhanced ability to automatically adjust and adapt to changing network conditions.

(continued)

Table 11. (*continued*)

Backlogs	Research challenges
– High implementation costs and complexity.	– Improve TCP's self-learning and adaptation capabilities in diverse network environments.
– Limited ability to adapt to sudden changes in network traffic.	– Optimize costs and simplify implementation of AQM algorithms.
– Compatibility and performance optimization between different threads are limited.	– Develop solutions that balance performance and optimize fairness between network flows.

5 Conclusion

In this study, we survey recent scientific research utilizing artificial intelligence (AI) for traffic control at routers. We provide a detailed analysis of the advantages and disadvantages of machine learning and deep learning algorithms, including supervised and unsupervised learning, as well as TCP congestion control algorithms and active queue management (AQM) mechanisms combined with AI techniques. From these analyses, the paper identifies and outlines the challenges that need to be addressed to ensure network performance at routers on the internet. These challenges not only involve enhancing the efficiency of current algorithms but also require the development and implementation of more advanced AI solutions to maintain stable and efficient network operations amid increasing and complex traffic.

Acknowledgment. We acknowledge the library resources provided by the Library of Nguyen Tat Thanh University.

References

1. Liu, T., Zhang, M., Zhu, J., Zheng, R., Liu, R., Wu, Q.: ACCP: adaptive congestion control protocol in named data networking based on deep learning. Neural Computing and Applications **31**, 4675–4683 (2018)
2. Perrier, V., Lochin, E., Tourneret, J.-Y., Kuhn, N., Gelard, P.: How attention deep learning can improve copa congestion control performance. HAL Open Sci. (2022)
3. Wang, K., Jing, Y., Liu, Y., Liu, X., Dimirovski, G.M.: Adaptive finite-time congestion controller design of TCP/AQM systems based on neural network and funnel control. Neural Comput. Appl. **32**, 9471–9478 (2019)
4. Jiang, H., et al.: When machine learning meets congestion control: a survey and comparison. Elsevier B.V (2021)
5. Geist, M., Jaeger, B.: Overview of TCP congestion control algorithms. Network **11** (2019)
6. Zhang, J., et al.: A survey of TCP congestion control algorithms. In: 2020 IEEE 5th International Conference on Signal and Image Processing (ICSIP). IEEE (2020)

7. Silva, A.P., et al.: A congestion control framework for delay-and disruption tolerant networks. Ad hoc networks 91 (2019)

8. Roy, A., Pachuau, J.L., Saha, A.K.: An overview of queuing delay and various delaybased algorithms in networks. Computing **103**(10) (2021)

9. Edwan, T.A., et al.: Revisiting legacy high-speed TCP congestion control variants: an optimisation-theoretic analysis of multi-mode TCP. Simul. Modell. Pract. Theory **118** (2022)

10. Noman, H.M., et al.: Improvement investigation of the TCP algorithms with avoiding network congestion based on OPNET. IOP Conf. Ser. Mat. Sci. Eng. **518**(5) (2019)

11. Welzl, M., et al.: Future internet congestion control: the diminishing feedback problem. IEEE Commun. Mag. **60**(9) (2022)

12. Kong, Y., Zang, H., Ma, X.: Improving TCP congestion control with machine intelligence. In: Proceedings of the 2018 Workshop on Network Meets AI & ML (2018)

13. Shi, H., Wang, J.: Intelligent TCP congestion control policy optimization. Appl. Sci. **13**(11) (2023)

14. Wang, Y., Wang, L., Dong, X.S.: An intelligent TCP congestion control method based on deep Q network. Future Internet (2021)

15. Jay, N., et al.: A deep reinforcement learning perspective on internet congestion control. In: International Conference on Machine Learning. PMLR (2019)

16. Khan, A.A., Farooq, M.U.: Classification of flow-based network applications using fuzzy logic (2023)

17. Gómez, J., Riaño, V.H., Ramirez-Gonzalez, G.: Traffic classification in IP networks through Machine Learning techniques in final systems. IEEE Access **11** (2023)

18. Sheikh, M.S., Peng, Y.: Procedures, criteria, and machine learning techniques for network traffic classification: a survey. IEEE Access **10** (2022)

19. Rajaboevich, G.S., et al.: Analysis of methods for measuring available bandwidth and classification of network traffic. Int. J. **8**(6) (2020)

20. Keerthipati. K., Karthika, R.A.: Active queue management techniques for congestion control in TCP communication networks: new prospective. Int. J. Innovat. Technol. Explor. Eng. (IJITEE) **9**(2-5) (2019)

21. Wang, Kun, et al. Adaptive fuzzy funnel congestion control for TCP/AQM network. ISA transactions. (2019)

22. Duran, G., et al.: Bifurcation analysis for Internet congestion. In: IEEE INFOCOM 2019-IEEE Conference on Computer Communications Workshops (INFOCOM WKSHPS), pp. 1073–1074. IEEE (2019)

23. Abu-Shareha, A.A.: Controlling delay at the router buffer using modified random early detection. Int. J. Comput. Networks Commun. (IJCNC) (2019)

24. Sabry, S.S., Kaittan, N.M.: Grey wolf optimizer based fuzzy-PI active queue management design for network congestion avoidance. Indonesian J. Electr. Eng. Comput. Sci. (2020)

25. Danladi, S.B., Ambursa, F.U.: DyRED: an enhanced random early detection based on a new adaptive congestion control. In; Proceedings of 2019 15th International Conference on Electronics, Computer and Computation (ICECCO) (2019)

26. Ma, L., et al.: Congestion tracking control for multi-router TCP/AQM network based on integral backstepping. Comput. Networks (2020)

27. Kar, S., et al.: PAQMAN: a principled approach to active queue management. arXiv preprint arXiv:2202.10352 (2022)

28. Berbek, M.I., Oglah, A.A.: Adaptive neuro-fuzzy controller trained by genetic-particle swarm for active queue management in internet congestion. Indonesian J. Electr. Eng. Comput. Sci. (2022)

29. Abood, L.H., Haitham, R.: Design an optimal fractional order PI controller for congestion avoidance in internet routers. Math. Modell. Eng. Probl. (2022)

30. Hassan, S.O., et al.: Improved random early detection congestion control algorithm for internet routers. Indonesian J. Electr. Eng. Comput. Sci. **28**(1), 384–395 (2022)
31. Abu-Shareha, A.A.: Integrated random early detection for congestion control at the router buffer. Comput. Syst. Sci. Eng. (2022)
32. Yousif, A.B., Hassan, H.J., Muttasher, G.: Intelligent parameter tuning using deep Q-network in adaptive queue management systems. Iraqi J. Comput. Commun. Control Syst. Eng. (IJCCCE) **22**(3) (2022)
33. Razmara, S., Barzamini, R., AlirezaIzadi, N.J.: A hybrid neural network approach for congestion control in TCP/IP Networks. Specialusis Ugdymas (2022)
34. Hassan, S.O., et al.: Quadratic exponential random early detection: a new enhanced random early detection-oriented congestion control algorithm for routers. Int. J. Electr. Comput. Eng. (2023)
35. Sneha, Y.V., et al.: Prediction of network congestion at router using machine learning technique. In: 2020 IEEE International Conference on Distributed Computing, VLSI, Electrical Circuits and Robotics (DISCOVER). IEEE (2020)
36. Sawada, T., et al.: TCP congestion control algorithm estimation by deep recurrent neural network and its application to web servers on the internet. Int. J. Adv. Networks Serv. **16**(1&2) (2023)
37. Abbasloo, S., Yen, C.-Y., Chao, H.J.: Classic meets modern: a pragmatic learning-based congestion control for the internet. In: Proceedings of the Annual conference of the ACM Special Interest Group on Data Communication on the applications, technologies, architectures, and protocols for computer communication (2020)
38. Xiao, K., Mao, S., Tugnait, J.K.: TCP-Drinc: Smart congestion control based on deep reinforcement learning. IEEE Access **7** (2019)
39. Postel, J.: Rfc0791: Internet protocol (1981)
40. Alkenani, J., Nassar, K.A.: Network monitoring measurements for quality of service: a review. Iraqi J. Electr. Electron. Eng. (2022)
41. Gomez, J., Riano, V.H., Ramirez-Gonzaiez, G.: Traffic classification in IP networks through Machine Learning techniques in final systems. IEEE Access **11**, 44932–44940 (2023)
42. Usama, M., et al.: Unsupervised machine learning for networking: techniques, applications and research challenges. IEEE Access (2019)
43. Isyaku, B., et al.: Dynamic routing and failure recovery approaches for efficient resource utilization in OpenFlow-SDN: a survey. IEEE Access **10** (2022)
44. Mousa, A.K., Abdullah, M.N.: A survey on load balancing, routing, and congestion in SDN. Eng. Technol. J **40**(10), 1284–1294 (2022)
45. Zhao, J., et al.: Network traffic classification for data fusion: a survey. Information Fusion (2021)
46. Huang, M., et al.: A queuing delay utilization scheme for on-path service aggregation in services-oriented computing networks. IEEE Access (2019)
47. Ricker, T., et al.: A machine learning approach to estimating queuing delay on a router over a single-hop path. In: ICC 2022-IEEE International Conference on Communications, pp. 2720–2725. IEEE (2022)
48. Salehin, K.M., Rojas-Cessa, R.: Scheme for measuring queueing delay of a router using probe-gap model: the single-hop case. IEEE Commun. Lett. **18**(4), 696–699 (2014)
49. Hu, Y., et al.: Network traffic classification based on external attention by IP packet header. arXiv preprint arXiv:2309.09440 (2023)
50. Nie, X., et al.: Dynamic TCP initial windows and congestion control schemes through reinforcement learning. IEEE J. Sel. Areas Commun. **37**(6), 1231–1247 (2019)
51. Zhang, T., Mao, S.: Machine learning for end-to-end congestion control. IEEE Commun. Mag. **58**(6), 52–57 (2020)

52. Xu, Z., et al.: Experience-driven congestion control: when multi-path TCP meets deep reinforcement learning. IEEE J. Sel. Areas Commun. (2019)
53. Emara, S., Li, B., Chen, Y.: Eagle: Refining congestion control by learning from the experts. In: IEEE INFOCOM. Conference on Computer Communications, pp. 676–685. IEEE (2020)
54. Adamu, A., et al.: Flexible random early detection algorithm for queue management in routers. In: Vishnevskiy, V.M., Samouylov, K.E., Kozyrev, D.V. (eds.) DCCN 2020. LNCS, vol. 12563, pp. 196–208. Springer, Cham (2020). https://doi.org/10.1007/978-3-030-66471-8_16
55. Kadhim, H.M., Oglah, A.A.: Congestion avoidance and control in internet router based on fuzzy AQM. Eng. Technol. J. **39**(2A), 233–247 (2021)
56. Liu, Z., et al.: An adaptive AQM algorithm based on a novel information compression model. IEEE Access **6**, 31180–31190 (2018)
57. Hamdi, M.M., et al.: A review on queue management algorithms in large networks. In: IOP Conference Series: Materials Science and Engineering. IOP Publishing, p. 012034. (2021)
58. Al-Allaf, A.F., Jabbar, A.I.A.: RED with reconfigurable maximum dropping probability. Int. J. Comput. Digit. Syst. **8**(01), 61–72 (2019)
59. Kar, S., et al.: PAQMAN: a principled approach to active queue management. arXiv 2022. arXiv preprint arXiv (2022)
60. Gimenez, A., et al.: New RED-type TCP-AQM algorithms based on beta distribution drop functions. Appl. Sci. (2022)
61. Mahawish, A.A., Hassan, H.J.: Survey on: a variety of AQM algorithm schemas and intelligent techniques developed for congestion control. Indones. J. Electr. Eng. Comput. Sci. (2021)
62. Hodaei, A., Babaie, S.: A survey on traffic management in software-defined networks: challenges, effective approaches, and potential measures. Wirel. Personal Commun. **118**(2), 1507–1534 (2021)
63. Salman, O., Elhajj, I.H., Kayssi, A., Chehab. A.: A review on machine learning–based approaches for internet traffic classification. Ann. Telecommun. (2020)
64. Naeem, S., et al.: An unsupervised machine learning-algorithms: comprehensive review. Int. J. Comput. Dig. Syst. **75**, 673–710 (2023)
65. Poorzare, R., Augé, A.C.: Challenges on the way of implementing TCP over 5G networks. IEEE Access **8**, 176393–176415 (2020)
66. Knott, J.: Improving TCP CUBIC congestion control with machine learning. In: Wellington Faculty of Engineering Symposium (2023)
67. Kabir, Md.A., Luo, X.: Unsupervised learning for network flow based anomaly detection in the era of deep learning. IEEE (2020)
68. Zhao, J., et al.: Network traffic classification for data fusion: a survey. Inf. Fusion **72**, 22–47 (2021)
69. James, G.J., et al.: Unsupervised learning. An introduction to statistical learning: with applications in Python. Springer, Cham (2023)

Steps Towards Modeling Collective Intelligence Using Linguistic Fuzzy Cognitive Maps

Nguyen Van Han[1]([⊠]) , Dang Van Pham[2]([⊠]) , Hoang Van Quy[1], and Tran Ngoc Dan[1]

[1] Faculty of Information Technology, Thuyloi University, 175 Tay Son - Dong Da District, Hanoi City, Vietnam
{nguyenvanhan,hoangvanquy,tranngocdan}@tlu.edu.vn
[2] Faculty of Information Technology, Nguyen Tat Thanh University, 300A Nguyen Tat Thanh street, Ward 13, District 4, Ho Chi Minh city, Vietnam
pvdang@ntt.edu.vn

Abstract. This research investigates the application of fuzzy logic and fuzzy cognitive maps (FCMs) in modeling and enhancing collective intelligence. Collective intelligence harnesses the combined knowledge and insights of a group, and this study explores how fuzzy logic and FCMs can effectively handle uncertainties, imprecisions, and dynamic interactions within such systems. The research aims to provide a comprehensive framework for understanding and improving collective decision-making processes.

Keywords: Collective Intelligence Modeling · Fuzzy Logic · Fuzzy Cognitive Maps · Collective Decision Making

1 Introduction

In the era of rapid technological advancements and complex decision-making processes, the quest for effective models of collective intelligence has become increasingly vital. Collective intelligence, defined as the ability of a group to solve problems and make decisions collaboratively, has gained prominence in various domains, including business, governance, and social systems. However, the inherent complexity and uncertainty associated with collective decision-making present challenges that demand sophisticated modeling approaches. In recent years, researchers have explored various methods to understand and model collective intelligence, ranging from traditional statistical approaches to more advanced computational techniques.

Combining fuzzy logic and fuzzy cognitive maps in the context of collective intelligence offers several advantages that enhance the modeling and understanding of complex decision-making processes within groups [1].

N. Van Han and D. Van Pham—Corresponding authors.

© ICST Institute for Computer Sciences, Social Informatics and Telecommunications Engineering 2026
Published by Springer Nature Switzerland AG 2026. All Rights Reserved
P. Cong Vinh et al. (Eds.): ICTCC 2024, LNICST 668, pp. 57–63, 2026.
https://doi.org/10.1007/978-3-032-12846-1_4

Specifically, fuzzy logic excels at handling uncertainty and imprecision in data and decision-making. It allows for the representation of vague and fuzzy concepts, which is crucial in capturing the inherent uncertainty present in collective intelligence scenarios [8–10]. While FCMs provide a graphical and intuitive representation of causal relationships within a system. By combining fuzzy logic with FCMs, the model gains the ability to handle both the imprecise nature of input data and the fuzzy nature of relationships among variables [2,11]. In [12,13] L. A. Zadeh, the father of fuzzy logic defined that:

$$\text{Fuzzy logic} = \text{computing with words}$$

Our research employs computing with words (CWW) and fuzzy cognitive maps, proven tools in dealing with uncertainty and complexity, to model the intricate relationships within collective decision-making scenarios. The combination of CWW's ability to handle imprecision and fuzzy cognitive maps' capability to represent causal relationships provides a comprehensive framework for capturing the nuances of group decision dynamics. By offering a step toward the implementation of CWW and fuzzy cognitive maps in modeling collective intelligence, this paper lays the groundwork for more robust and adaptive decision support systems.

The remainder of this paper is organized as follows: Sect. 2 provides a comprehensive review of the literature related to collective intelligence and fuzzy logic applications. In Sect. 3, we detail the methodology, outlining the steps involved in modeling collective intelligence using fuzzy logic and fuzzy cognitive maps. Finally, Sect. 4 concludes the paper with implications for future research and practical applications.

2   Preliminary and Literature Review

In the domain of computing with words, where linguistic variables and fuzzy logic are employed to model human-like reasoning, hedge algebra becomes a powerful tool. It allows for the manipulation of linguistic expressions in a way that aligns with human reasoning processes.

2.1   Hedge Algebra

Hedge algebra is an algebraic structure used in fuzzy logic and linguistic variable modeling, particularly for handling linguistic terms and their modifications by hedges such as "very," "more or less, ... It provides a formal framework for representing and reasoning about linguistic values and their modifications. HA. was introduced to handle the imprecision and vagueness inherent in linguistic terms, particularly in fuzzy logic systems.

- Linguistic variable domain: A linguistic variable X has a domain of linguistic terms $T(X)$ such as $\{low, medium, high\}$.
- Hedges (Modifiers): A set of hedges $H = \{h_1, h_2, \dots\}$, where each hedge represents a modification like "very," "slightly," ....

– Ordering Relation: Hedge Algebra imposes a partial or total ordering on the set of linguistic values. For example, *"cold"* might be less than *"warm,"* and *"warm"* might be less than *"hot."* Applying hedges modifies this ordering.

Definition 1. *[6] A hedge algebra (ℍ𝔸) is Tuples*

$$\mathbb{HA} = (X, G, C, H, \le)$$

where $H \ne \emptyset$, $G = \{c^+,\ c^-\}$, $C = \{0, W, 1\}$. Domain of X is $\mathscr{W} = Dom(X) = \{\delta c \mid c \in G,\ \delta \in H^* (hedge\ string\ over\ H)\}$, $\{\mathscr{W}, \le\}$ is a POSET (partial order set) and $x = h_n h_{n-1} \dots h_1 c$ Is referred to as the canonical string corresponding to the linguistic variable x.

Example 1. Fuzzy subset X is *TEMPERATURE*, $G = \{c^+ = \mathsf{high};\ c^- = \mathsf{low}\}$, $H = \{slightly; very\}$ so term-set of linguistic variable *Age X* is $\mathscr{W}(X)$ or $\mathscr{W}$ for short:
$\mathscr{W} = \{very\ very\ \mathsf{high}, slightly\ very\ \mathsf{high}, \dots, slightly\ very\ \mathsf{low} \dots\}$

Fuzziness properties of elements in ℍ𝔸, specified by (fuzziness measure) [5] as follows:

Definition 2. *A mapping $: \mathscr{W} \to [0,1]$ is said to be the fuzziness measure of $\mathscr{W}$ if:*

1. $\sum_{c \in \{c^+, c^-\}} (c) = 1$, $(0) = (w) = (1) = 0$.
2. $\sum_{h_i \in H} (h_i x) = (x)$, $x = h_n h_{n-1} \dots h_1 c$, *the canonical form.*
3. $(h_n h_{n-1} \dots h_1 c) = \prod_{i=1}^{n} (h_i) \times \mu(c)$.
4. *for $\forall\ x,\ y \in \mathscr{W}$, for $\forall\ h \in H$*

$$\frac{(hx)}{(x)} = \frac{(hy)}{(y)}$$

This ratio does not depend on specific factors and is called fuzziness measure of hedge h , denoted by $\mu(h)$

2.2 Fuzzy Cogntive Maps

A Fuzzy Cognitive Map (FCM), which was introduced by B. Kosko [7] is a graph-based model that represents the relationships and influences among a set of concepts or variables, where fuzzy logic is used to handle the uncertainty and vagueness of these relationships. Each concept in the map is connected to other concepts through weighted edges, and these weights are typically fuzzy values that represent the strength and nature (positive or negative) of the influence between concepts. The belief about how strongly one concept influences another is represented by a fuzzy weight on the connection (edge) between the two concepts. This weight is a fuzzy number, often in the range of $[-1, 1]$, where:

– Positive values represent positive influence (one concept increases the value of the other).

- Negative values represent negative influence (one concept decreases the value of the other).
- Values closer to 0 represent weaker beliefs about the influence.

The state transform equation for updating the activation level of concept C_i at the next time step $t+1$ is generally given by:

$$C_i^{(t+1)} = f(\sum_{j=1}^{N} C_j^{(t)} e_{ji}) \tag{1}$$

Where:

- $C_i^{(t+1)}$ is the new activation level of concept C_i at time $t+1$
- $C_i^{(t1)}$ is the activation level of concept C_i at time t
- e_{ji} is the weight representing the influence of concept C_j on concept C_i

3 Towards Fuzzy Modeling of Air Pollution Evolution

FCMs find applications in diverse areas. One notable application is in decision support systems, where FCMs are employed to model and analyze complex decision-making processes involving multiple variables. The ability of FCMs to capture the fuzzy nature of human cognition makes them well-suited for representing expert knowledge and reasoning under uncertainty [2,11]. Additionally, FCMs are utilized in machine learning tasks, particularly for pattern recognition and classification in collective intelligence [1].

The advanced use of hedge algebra in modeling fuzzy cognitive maps is believed to significantly enhance the capabilities of FCMs. By providing a more flexible and nuanced way to handle linguistic variables, hedge algebra allows for the development of more interpretable, adaptable, and human-friendly models. This is particularly important in fields where decisions must be made under uncertainty and where the interpretability of the model is as important as its accuracy (Fig. 1). The combination of HA into model FCM produces model linguistic cognitive map (LCM). This model has many advanced applications in artificial intelligence [3,4].

Table 1. Domains conversion

Effect	Value	Domain of $\mathcal{W}$
	1	1
high positive (+++)	0.5	very high (vh)
middle positive (++)	0.25	more high (mh)
	0	$\mathcal{W}$
high negative (−)	−0.25	more low (ml)
high negative (—)	−0.5	very low (vl)
	−1	0

The Table 1 converts numerical domain to linguistic domain on $\mathcal{W}$. The Table 2 shows all casual relation between all fuzzy concepts of pollution evolution.

Table 2. Domain of words

	CO	NO	NO_2	O_3	SO_2	AirTemp	RH	PR	SR	SUN	WS	WD	RF
CO		vh	mh	vl	mh	$\mathcal{W}$	$\mathcal{W}$	$\mathcal{W}$	$\mathcal{W}$	$\mathcal{W}$	$\mathcal{W}$	$\mathcal{W}$	ml
NO	vh		mh	vl	mh	ml	mh	$\mathcal{W}$	$\mathcal{W}$	$\mathcal{W}$	ml	$\mathcal{W}$	vl
NO_2	vh	vh		vl	mh	$\mathcal{W}$	$\mathcal{W}$	$\mathcal{W}$	$\mathcal{W}$	$\mathcal{W}$	ml	$\mathcal{W}$	vl
O_3	vl	vl	vl		ml	mh	vl	$\mathcal{W}$	$\mathcal{W}$	$\mathcal{W}$	vh	$\mathcal{W}$	vl
SO_2	vh	vh	mh	vl		vl	$\mathcal{W}$	mh	$\mathcal{W}$	$\mathcal{W}$	ml	$\mathcal{W}$	vl
$AirTemp$	$\mathcal{W}$	$\mathcal{W}$	mh	vh	ml		vl	$\mathcal{W}$	mh	mh	$\mathcal{W}$	$\mathcal{W}$	ml
RH	mh	vh	$\mathcal{W}$	vl	$\mathcal{W}$	vl		$\mathcal{W}$	vl	vl	ml	$\mathcal{W}$	vh
PR	$\mathcal{W}$	$\mathcal{W}$	$\mathcal{W}$	$\mathcal{W}$	vh	vl	$\mathcal{W}$		$\mathcal{W}$	$\mathcal{W}$	$\mathcal{W}$	ml	vl
SR	$\mathcal{W}$	$\mathcal{W}$	$\mathcal{W}$	$\mathcal{W}$	$\mathcal{W}$	mh	vl	$\mathcal{W}$		vh	mh	$\mathcal{W}$	vl
SUN	$\mathcal{W}$	$\mathcal{W}$	mh	mh	$\mathcal{W}$	mh	vl	$\mathcal{W}$	vh		mh	$\mathcal{W}$	vl
WS	vl	vl	ml	vh	ml	$\mathcal{W}$	ml	$\mathcal{W}$	mh	mh		$\mathcal{W}$	$\mathcal{W}$
WD	mh	mh	vh	ml	$\mathcal{W}$	$\mathcal{W}$	$\mathcal{W}$	vl	mh	mh	ml		$\mathcal{W}$
RF	vl	vl	vl	vl	vl	ml	mh	vl	vl	vl	$\mathcal{W}$	$\mathcal{W}$	

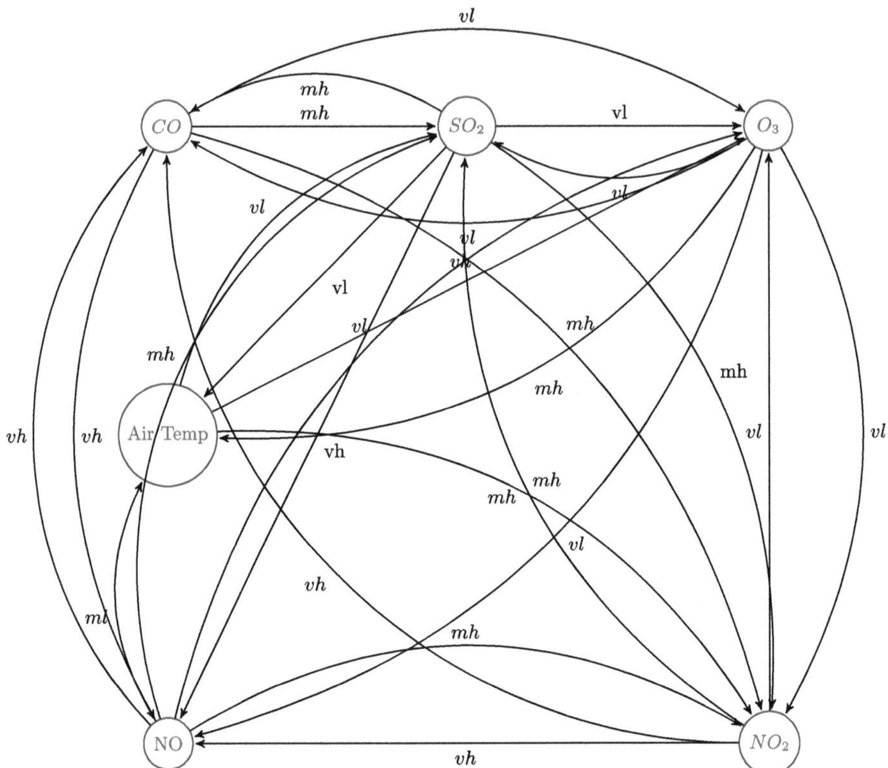

Fig. 1. Linguistic cognitive map models air pollution evolution

4   Conclusion and Forthcoming Study

The paper study of modeling collective intelligence using linguistic fuzzy cognitive maps.

- Study of modeling fuzzy system based on hedge algebra
- Study of applying linguistic cognitive map in modeling of air pollution evolution

In the future, two studies will be:

- Research on applying fuzzy system in agriculture and temprature areas.
- Develop algorithms for modeling and reasoning on linguistic fuzzy cognitive maps.

References

1. Anezakis, VD., Dermetzis, K., Iliadis, L., Spartalis, S.: Fuzzy cognitive maps for long-term prognosis of the evolution of atmospheric pollution, based on climate change scenarios: the case of Athens. In: Computational Collective Intelligence, pp. 175–186 (2016)
2. Glykas, M.: Fuzzy Cognitive Maps, Advances in Theory. Springer, Tools and Applications (2010)
3. Han, N.V., Hao, N.C., Vinh, P.C.: Toward aggregating fuzzy graphs: a model theory approach. In: Context-Aware Systems and Applications, and Nature of Computation and Communication. ICCASA 2019, ICTCC 2019. Lecture Notes of the Institute for Computer Sciences, Social Informatics and Telecommunications Engineering, vol. 298, pp. 215–222 (2019)
4. Han, N.V., Vinh, P.C.: Modeling with words based on hedge algebra. In: 7th EAI International Conference, ICCASA 2018 and 4th EAI International Conference, ICTCC 2018, vol. 266, 211–217 (2018)
5. Ho, N.C., Son, T.T., Khang, T.D., Viet, L.X.: Fuzziness measure, quantified semantic mapping and interpolative method of approximate reasoning in medical expert systems. J. Comput. Sci. Cybern. **18**(3), 237–252 (2002)
6. Ho, N.C., Wechler, W.: Hedge algebras: an algebraic approach to structure of sets of linguistic truth values. Fuzzy Sets Syst. **35**(3), 281–293 (1990)
7. Kosko, B.: Fuzzy cognitive MPAs. Int. J. Man-Mach. Stud. **24**, 65–75 (1986)
8. Zadeh, L.A.: The concept of a linguistic variable and its applications to approximate reasoning. Inf. Sci. **8**(3), 199–249 (1975)
9. Zadeh, L.A.: Fuzzy-set-theoretic interpretation of linguistic hedges. J. Cybern. **2**, 4–34 (1977)
10. Zadeh, L.A.: Computing with words - Principal Concepts and Ideas. Studies in Fuzziness and Soft Computing. Springer (2012)
11. Elpiniki, I.: Papageorgiou. Fuzzy Cognitive Maps for Applied Science and Engineering From Fundamentals to Extensions and Learning Algorithms. Springer-Verlag Berlin Heidelberg (2014)
12. Zadeh, L.A.: Fuzzy logic = computing with words. IEEE Trans. Fuzzy Syst. **4**, 103–111 (1996)
13. Zadeh, L.A., Kacprzyk, J.: Computing with Word in Information Intelligent System 1. Springer-Verlag BBerlin Heidelberg GmbH (1999)

Toward Modeling Adaptive Neuro-Fuzzy Inference System Based on Hedge Algebra

Nguyen Van Han[1]($\boxtimes$) ![ORCID], Dang Van Pham[2]($\boxtimes$) ![ORCID], and Tran Ngoc Dan[1]

[1] Faculty of Information Technology, Thuyloi University, 175 Tay Son - Dong Da District, Hanoi City, Vietnam
{nguyenvanhan,tranngocdan}@tlu.edu.vn
[2] Faculty of Information Technology, Nguyen Tat Thanh University,300A Nguyen Tat Thanh street, Ward 13, District 4, Ho Chi Minh City, Vietnam
pvdang@ntt.edu.vn

Abstract. This study aims to develop an Adaptive Neuro-Fuzzy Inference System (ANFIS) that integrates Hedge Algebra to handle uncertainties and linguistic variables more effectively. Hedge Algebra is used to enhance the interpretability and adaptability of the system. The proposed model incorporates Hedge Algebra to manage the semantic meanings of linguistic terms within the fuzzy inference system. The adaptability of the system is achieved through reinforcement learning mechanisms, enabling it to refine its fuzzy rules and membership functions dynamically. This research bridges the gap between traditional fuzzy systems and Hedge Algebra, offering a robust framework for applications requiring nuanced linguistic reasoning and adaptability.

Keywords: Adaptive Neuro-Fuzzy Inference System (ANFIS) · Hedge Algebra (HA) · Fuzzy Systems

1 Introduction

Artificial intelligence (AI) has seen significant advances in recent years, leading to the development of complex systems that can simulate human reasoning and decision-making. Among these, Neuro-Fuzzy Inference Systems (NFIS) [3] have emerged as a powerful tool for solving problems where both learning capabilities and interpretability are crucial. NFIS combines the adaptive learning capabilities of neural networks with the human-like reasoning provided by fuzzy logic, making it particularly useful in domains where data is uncertain, imprecise, or described in linguistic terms.

Fuzzy logic was first introduced by Zadeh in 1965 [4] as a means of handling the vagueness and ambiguity inherent in human reasoning and natural language. It uses linguistic variables instead of binary true/false values, allowing for a more flexible and human-like approach to reasoning. However, traditional

P. Cong Vinh et al. (Eds.): ICTCC 2024, LNICST 668, pp. 64–69, 2026.
https://doi.org/10.1007/978-3-032-12846-1_5

fuzzy systems often struggle with the interpretability of linguistic terms and the adaptability required in dynamic environments.

To address these challenges, the Adaptive Neuro-Fuzzy Inference System (ANFIS) was developed, which integrates fuzzy logic with neural networks. ANFIS can learn and adapt by adjusting its fuzzy rules and membership functions through training, similar to a neural network. However, despite its success, traditional ANFIS models can sometimes fall short in effectively handling linguistic variables, particularly when the semantics of these variables are complex or context-dependent.

Hedge Algebra (HA) [1,2], a mathematical approach developed by Ho and Wechler in the early 1990 s, offers a solution to this problem. HA provides a formal framework for representing and processing linguistic variables, enhancing the precision and interpretability of fuzzy systems. Unlike conventional fuzzy logic, which relies on membership functions to quantify linguistic terms, HA uses algebraic structures to capture the inherent ordering and relationships between these terms. This allows for a more nuanced representation of linguistic variables, making HA particularly suitable for applications requiring detailed linguistic reasoning. The rest of the paper is organized as follows: Sect. 2 reviews related work on Adaptive Neuro-Fuzzy Inference System, highlighting the research gap that this paper addresses. Section 3 presents the theoretical framework, formally defining hedge algebra and its integration into ANFIS, describes the architecture of the proposed linguistic ANFIS model, detailing each component and its role. Section 4 summaries outlines the corollary as well as future work.

2   Preliminary and Literature Review

This section summarizes the knowledge related to the article. These include hedge algebra (HA) and Adaptive Neuro-Fuzzy Inference System.

2.1   Hedge Algebra and Traditional Fuzzy Logic

Traditional fuzzy logic relies on membership functions to represent the degrees of truth or falsehood of a linguistic variable. While effective, this approach can be limited in handling the nuanced meanings of linguistic terms, especially when these terms are modified by hedges. Hedge Algebra addresses this limitation by providing a more formal and mathematical means of representing these modifications. The algebraic structure of HA captures the relationships between base terms and their hedges, allowing for a more precise interpretation of linguistic variables. This has led to HA being seen as a powerful complement to fuzzy set theory in applications where linguistic terms are critical.

- Linguistic variables: A linguistic variable X has a domain of linguistic terms $T(X)$ such as {high, low}.
- Hedges (Modifiers): A set of hedges $H = \{h_1, h_2, \ldots\}$, where each hedge represents a modification like "more or less," "slightly," ....

– Ordering Relation: Hedge Algebra imposes a partial or total ordering on the set of linguistic values. For example, *"cold"* might be less than *"warm,"* and *"warm"* might be less than *"hot."* Applying hedges modifies this ordering.

Definition 1. *[2] A hedge algebra (*$\mathbb{HA}$*) is Tuples*

$$\mathbb{HA} = (X, G, C, H, \leq)$$

where $H \neq \emptyset$, $G = \{c^+, c^-\}$, $C = \{0, W, 1\}$. *Domain of* X *is* $\mathbb{L} = Dom(X) = \{\delta c \mid c \in G, \delta \in H^* (hedge\ string\ over\ H)\}$, $\{\mathbb{L}, \leq\}$ *is a POSET (partial order set) and* $x = h_n h_{n-1} \ldots h_1 c$ *Is referred to as the canonical string corresponding to the linguistic variable* x.

Example 1. Fuzzy subset X *is SPEED (of cars)* , $G = \{c^+ = $ high; $c^- = $ low$\}$, $H = \{absolutely; very\}$ so term-set of linguistic variable *SPEED* X is $\mathbb{L}(X)$ or $\mathbb{L}$ for short:
$\mathbb{L} = \{very\ very$ high, *absolutely very* high, $\ldots$, *absolutely very* low $\ldots\}$

Fuzziness properties of elements in $\mathbb{HA}$, specified by fm (fuzziness measure) [1] as follows:

Definition 2. *A mapping* $fm : \mathbb{L} \to [0, 1]$ *is said to be the fuzziness measure of* $\mathbb{L}$ *if:*

1. $\sum_{c \in \{c^+, c^-\}} fm(c) = 1,\ fm(0) = fm(w) = fm(1) = 0.$
2. $\sum_{h_i \in H} fm(h_i x) = fm(x),\ x = h_n h_{n-1} \ldots h_1 c$, *the canonical form.*
3. $fm(h_n h_{n-1} \ldots h_1 c) = \prod_{i=1}^{n} fm(h_i) \times \mu(c).$
4. *for* $\forall\ x,\ y \in \mathbb{L},\ for\ \forall\ h \in H$

$$\frac{fm(hx)}{fm(x)} = \frac{fm(hy)}{fm(y)}$$

This ratio does not depend on specific factors and is called fuzziness measure of hedge h *, denoted by* $\mu(h)$

2.2   Adaptive Neuro-Fuzzy Inference System

The Adaptive Neuro-Fuzzy Inference System (ANFIS) [3] is a hybrid intelligent system that combines the learning capabilities of artificial neural networks (ANNs) with the human-like reasoning style of fuzzy logic. Introduced by Jang in 1993, ANFIS leverages the strengths of both paradigms to model complex, nonlinear systems effectively. The core idea is to use a fuzzy inference system (FIS) to represent the problem space and an ANN to optimize the parameters of the FIS, such as membership functions and fuzzy rules, through learning from data.

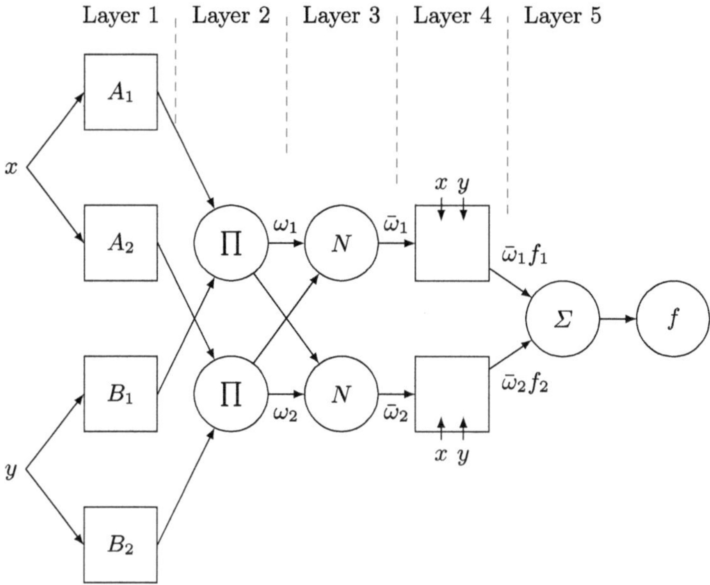

Fig. 1. ANFIS model

The Fig. 1 depicts a structure ANFIS which presents of two rules [5]:

$$R_1 : \text{If } x_1 \text{ is } A_1 \text{and } x_2 \text{ is } B_1 \text{ then} y = f_1(x)$$
$$R_2 : \text{If } x_1 \text{ is } A_2 \text{and } x_2 \text{ is } B_2 \text{ then} y = f_2(x)$$

In whicn $x = (x_1, x_2)$ is numerical input and A_1, A_2, B_1, B_2 are fuzzy sets. The outputs:

$$\omega_i = A_i(x_1)B_i(x_2), \ i = \overline{1,2}$$
$$\overline{\omega_i} = \frac{\omega_i}{\omega_1 + \omega_2}$$
$$f = \frac{\sum_{i=1}^{2} \overline{\omega_i} \times f_i}{\sum_{i=1}^{2} \overline{\omega_i}}$$

3   Toward Modeling Linguistic ANFIS

The combination of ANFIS with HA represents a significant advancement in the field of fuzzy logic and soft computing. This integration leverages the strengths of both ANFIS and HA to address some of the inherent challenges in traditional fuzzy systems, particularly in the areas of linguistic variable representation, interpretability, and adaptability.

3.1   Definition and Architectural Model

Definition 3. *A linguistic ANFIS (L-ANFIS) is an ANFIS which consists of five layers*

 - *Input set $\mathcal{I} : [\, I_1 \; I_2 \ldots I_n]^T \in \mathbb{L}^n$*
 - *Output set $\mathcal{O}$: The output equation of fuzzy system using centroid defuzzifier is expressed as:*

$$\mathcal{O} = \frac{\sum_{i=1}^{2} \overline{\mathcal{O}_i} \times f_i}{\sum_{i=1}^{2} \overline{\mathcal{O}_i}} \tag{1}$$

The Fig. 2 presents a L-ANFIS, which consists of five layers In whicn $x = (x_1, x_2) \in \mathbb{L}$ is numerical input and A_1, A_2, B_1, $B_2 \subset \mathbb{L}$ are fuzzy sets for two rules:

$$R_1 : \text{If } x_1 \text{ is } A_1 \text{and } x_2 \text{ is } B_1 \text{ then } y = f_1(x)$$
$$R_2 : \text{If } x_1 \text{ is } A_2 \text{and } x_2 \text{ is } B_2 \text{ then } y = f_2(x)$$

3.2   Algorithm and Applications

This section provides the pseudocode for the input, output, and computational processes of the L-ANFIS network, as shown in Algorithm 1. The application of L-ANFIS in classification tasks is determined by the value of the delta function.

Algorithm 1. L-ANFIS system computational algorithm

    Input: Input vectors $\mathcal{I} \in \mathbb{L}$ and wights $\mathcal{W} \in \mathbb{L}$
    Output: Value $\mathcal{O}$
 1: **for** $i \leftarrow 1$ to n **do**   ▷ Initialize values for *fuzzy concept*
 2:    $I_i \in \mathbb{L}$
 3: **end for**
 4: $\mathcal{O}_j \leftarrow 1$ ▷ Initial condition
 5: **for** $j \leftarrow 1$ to M **do**   ▷ Computing for bocks $j = \overline{1, M}$
 6:    $\mathcal{O}_j \leftarrow \mathcal{O}_j \wedge A_j(x_1) \wedge B_j(x_2) \ldots$
 7:    $\overline{\mathcal{O}_j} \leftarrow \dfrac{\mathcal{O}_j}{\mathcal{O}_1 \vee \mathcal{O}_2 \vee \ldots \vee \mathcal{O}_j}$
 8:    $\mathcal{O} = \dfrac{\overline{\mathcal{O}_j} \wedge f_j}{\overline{\mathcal{O}_i}}$
 9: **end for**
10: **return** $\mathcal{O}$

Example 2. With $M = 2$, the outputs for the model of Fig. 2 are:

$$\mathcal{O}_i = A_i(x_1) \wedge B_i(x_2), \; i = \overline{1,2}$$
$$\overline{\mathcal{O}_i} = \frac{\mathcal{O}_i}{\mathcal{O}_1 \vee \mathcal{O}_2}$$
$$\mathcal{O} = \frac{\bigvee_{i=1}^{2} \overline{\mathcal{O}_i} \wedge f_i}{\bigvee_{i=1}^{2} \overline{\mathcal{O}_i}}$$

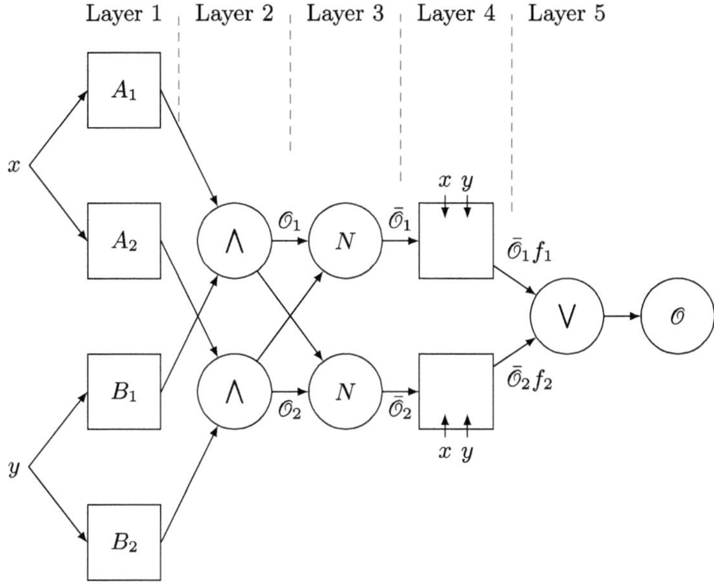

Fig. 2. A Linguistic ANFIS model

4   Conclusion and Forthcoming Study

The article proposes a modeling with word based on fuzzy system and neural network

– The linguistic adaptive neuro-fuzzy inference system.
– The algorithm to calulation of input and output with five layers of network.

In the future, two studies will be:

– Research on modeling and reasoning methods on deep structures of linguistic adaptive neuro-fuzzy inference system.
– Research on applying for L-ANFIS in artificial Intelligence.

References

1. Ho, N.C., Son, T.T., Khang, T.D., Viet, L.X.: Fuzziness measure, quantified semantic mapping and interpolative method of approximate reasoning in medical expert systems. J. Comput. Sci. Cybern. **18**(3), 237–252 (2002)
2. Ho, N.C., Wechler, W.: Hedge algebras: an algebraic approach to structure of sets of linguistic truth values. Fuzzy Sets Syst. **35**(3), 281–293 (1990)
3. Jang, J.R.: ANFIS: adaptive-network-based fuzzy inference system **24**(3), 665–685 (1993)
4. Zadeh, L.A.: Fuzzy sets. Inf. Control **8**, 338–353 (1965)
5. Prasad, N.R., Nguyen, H.T., Walker, C.L.: A First Course in Fuzzy and Neural Control. Chapman and Hall/CRC (2024)

Analyzing and Comparing the Stream Theory: A Review

Dang Van Pham[1,2,3](✉) ⓘ, Vinh Cong Phan[1,2,3](✉) ⓘ, and Trong Toan Tran[1,2] ⓘ

[1] Graduate University of Science and Technology, Vietnam Academy of Science and Technology, Hanoi, Vietnam
{pvdang,pcvinh}@ntt.edu.vn
[2] Institute of Applied Mechanics and Informatics, Vietnam Academy of Science and Technology, Ho Chi Minh City, Vietnam
[3] Faculty of Information Technology, Nguyen Tat Thanh University, Ho Chi Minh City, Vietnam

Abstract. This is a consideration paper on the applying of the stream theory for the era of big data analytics. The stream theory that includes the stream algebra and the stream coalgebra, and this theory plays a very important role in mathematics and computer science, particularly in the analytics of big data in generally and big data in livestream (BDL) in particularly. Both the stream algebra and the stream coalgebra are applied to solving problems involving structured, semi-structured, and unstructured data. This research focuses on analyzing and comparing the stream theory based on characteristic criteria. This research constructs eight tables to analyze and compare the characteristic criteria that the stream theory has contributed from the past to the present. Through these analytical and comparative tables, we can gain an extensive understanding of the contributions of the stream theory and help them envision the development of the stream theory in the future.

Keywords: Stream theory · stream algebra · stream coalgebra · big data in livestream (BDL)

1 Introduction

Big data now exists in many complex forms and is constantly changing over time. Generated big data no longer have a standard format or structure like the conventional ones and cannot be processed using relational models. Big data come in the form of text, emails, images, weblogs, videos, and so on resulting in a surge of new data types. Thus, this complexity of big data is expressed in three structured aspects in the following. *Aspect 1* is structured data that uses a predefined data model with existing model levels and values already filled in available (data tables, excel files or electronic forms). *Aspect 2* is unstructured data that has not structured, not predefined data model, making it more difficult to collect, process, and analyze (text documents, audio, photos, social media posts, or video files). *Aspect 3* is semi-structured data that it is hybrid form that does not reside in a relational database but still has some organizational properties that make

P. Cong Vinh et al. (Eds.): ICTCC 2024, LNICST 668, pp. 70–109, 2026.
https://doi.org/10.1007/978-3-032-12846-1_6

it easier to analyze than unstructured data (email stores, XML or NoSQL) [1–8]. The stream theory is an importance role in applied to solving problems related to structured types in Fig. 1. In which, big data in livestream (BDL) also exists in many different formats and is classified as unstructured data appearing on livestream platforms but currently, we have not found a mathematical platform that studies, defines, explains, interprets and proves the operating mechanisms of BDL has yet to be discovered [9].

Analytical tables analyzing and comparing several of the research work related to the stream theory are needed to be surveyed. We conduct analysis in the next subsections of this paper to help researchers gain insight into the types of data structure and operating systems that the stream theory has contributed. The objective of this paper is to systematize several of the research work related to the stream theory including the stream algebra and the stream coalgebra with eight tables of analyzing and comparing through characteristic criteria. These tables help us visualize the major contributions that the stream theory makes in the analytics of big data in generally and big data in livestream (BDL) in particularly.

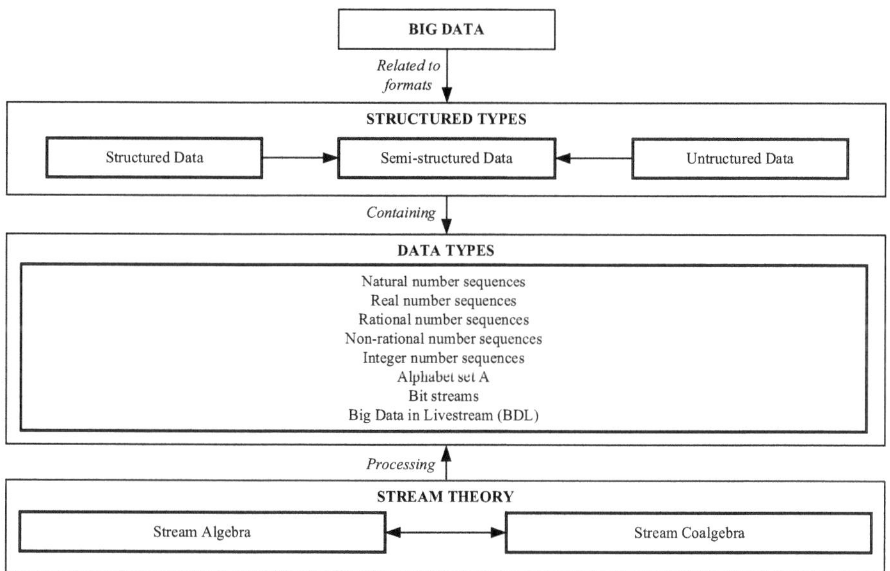

Fig. 1. Big data of structured types for the stream theory in big data analytics

The structure of this paper is organized as follows. Section 1 focuses on describing the problem, motivations and objectives to be solved by stream theory. Section 2 presents the systematization of related work, gives to comment and propose analyzing and comparing of the stream theory via characteristic criteria. Section 3 proposes eight analysis and comparison tables for stream theory. Section 4 analyzes the strengths and shortcomings of the stream theory. Section 5 conducts the discussions. Section 6 outlines the conclusions. Finally, there are references.

2 Related Works

2.1 The Stream Algebra

Large-scale computer vision systems use stream-based concepts to enhance data streams more visually. Helala et al. [10] provide a formal algebraic foundation for describing and optimizing computer vision pipeline mechanisms for image and video data streams. This algebra handles feedback control and offers an abstract optimization method for computer vision pipelines, including online parameter optimization. Mauricio et al. [11] study basic stream operators in stream algebra for real and natural number sequences, including sequential and parallel composition, delay, synchronized parallel composition, restriction, transformation, reverse, and derivative.

Streams are infinite objects with extensive theoretical development due to their relevance in mathematics and computer science. They manifest as numerical expansions, data sequences, formal power series, limit sequences, dynamic system behavior, formal languages, and ongoing computations. Stream differential equations, a coinductive method, specify streams and stream operators. Helle et al. [12] have categorized various formats of behavioral differential equations, their solutions, and the types of streams they define. Giorgio et al. [13] apply stream algebra and coalgebra to model the syntax and semantics of stochastic processes with continuously changing states, consistent with unit measure spaces. They propose a rule-like formulation for structured operational semantics to achieve fully abstract general semantics, using behavioral equivalence. This specification includes measures to describe finite measures, integrating both the syntax and interpretation of these measurement terms into the rule formulation.

The state transition structure $\alpha : X \to X^A$ of a deterministic automaton, where each state has exactly one output event, can be viewed through the lenses of both algebra and coalgebra. Ballester et al. [14] leverage this algebra and coalgebra duality to study equations and coequations from a general perspective. For any given automaton (X, α), they define two new automata: free (X, α) and cofree (X, α). These automata represent the largest and smallest sets of equations satisfied by (X, α), respectively. Both constructions are shown to be functorial. The main finding of their work is that the restrictions of free and cofree automata correspond to the preformation forms of languages and the quotient A^*/C of A^* by a congruence relation C, forming a dual equivalence. Filippo et al. [15] employ universal algebra and coalgebra to minimize finite automata, providing a general approach and demonstrating correctness. They derive algorithms to obtain a language-equivalent minimal automaton from a weighted and nondeterministic automaton, where a state can have multiple output events. Milad et al. [16] use stream calculus and stream circuits to define and prove properties of stream operators such as splitting, partitioning, projecting, and merging on data streams, utilizing behavioral differential equations and coinductive proof principles. These operators are extensively used in data stream programming and stream processing languages.

The calculus of streams of sequential sequences, represented as $1 \perp -$ sequences, involves infinite sequences of $\{0, 1, \perp\}$ with most entries being $\perp$. This calculus is used in real number calculations within the unit interval $\mathbb{I}$, embedded in the stream set $\Sigma_{\perp,1}^{\omega}$ of sequences. Real functions on $\mathbb{I}$ can be expressed as input-output programs, with sequences as inputs and outputs, utilizing operators for addition and multiplication of these sequences [17]. Ralf [18] suggests an alternative to the induction method, with limited scope and unique solutions for stream equations. This approach provides a balanced proof technique for the same domain. The research revisits previous theories and finite computations, generating functions using streams and their operators. It focuses on recursion elimination and binary stream sequences, leveraging the rich structure of streams. As streams are a practical functor, their operators and properties can be readily translated, enhancing the architecture of streams and their operators, implemented by a specific class.

Stream differential equations are used to define infinite streams. Kupke et al. [19] ensure that any system of equations fitting their syntactic format has a unique solution, precisely determining stream functions. They use non-standard stream calculus with different basic operators from head and tail to define and discuss streams and stream functions. Stream circuits optimally represent streams or stream functions computed by finite-dimensional linear systems. Stefan [20] introduces a calculus that ensures soundness and completeness for reasoning about the semantic equivalence of finite closed stream circuits. To prove this, the author builds on previous research providing a sound and complete calculus for coalgebras for endofunctors on the category of sets, requiring a syntactic specification of the final locally finite dimensional coalgebra.

Stream computation is a growing area in computer science and mathematics. Some approaches use stream programming languages and rewriting systems to formally represent computational programs on data streams. However, no stream calculus has been proposed yet, which would allow for more general research without a fixed reduction strategy, making it more modular and compositional than stream rewriting systems. A new stream rewriting system is typically designed for each specific problem [21]. A recent survey [22] examines stream programming languages, which are used to write applications for analyzing data streams. With the big data era, data streams have grown significantly, necessitating stream processing applications. The survey introduces several languages for this purpose, explains fundamental principles, and outlines remaining challenges.

In [23], the authors examine operators like partitioning, projecting, merging, and splitting in stream data programming and processing languages. Using stream calculus and stream circuits, they define and prove the properties of these operators with behavioral differential equations and coinductive proofs. They explore invariance in patterned streams, showing that extended stream circuits with gates for splitting and merging can realize certain algebraic streams, surpassing ordinary stream circuits. In [24], input data stream programming and scheduling are studied, proving behavior equivalence in the synthesis process regardless of scheduling changes. In [25], coinductive stream calculus is applied to signal flow graphs, addressing memory (registers or delay units) and infinite behavior (feedback circuits).

In [26], the author analyzes four algebraic structures on bitstreams underlying digital circuits, identifying one structure with two-operand numbers that characterize rational streams in linear digital circuits. In [27], the author combines basic stream circuits, proving that a stream $\rho \in \mathbb{R}^\omega$ is rational if generated by a finite stream circuit. Using the final coalgebraic structure on streams of real numbers, a coinductive calculus of streams is developed, focusing on stream derivatives with coinductive proofs and definitions.

Applications include differential equations, continuous fractions, and problems in discrete and combinatorial mathematics [28]. Tucker et al. [29] describe a stream algebra A, where a stream is an infinite sequence from A. They study functions computing on streams following A, showing how parallel computing models on A can be adapted for new computational models on the stream algebra.

2.2 The Stream Coalgebra

In [30], the authors explore the relationship between polynomials, differential equations, and streams over a field $\mathbb{K}$, both algebraically and coalgebraically. They introduce (F, G)-products on streams, showing that the stream derivative of such a product can be expressed as a polynomial function of streams and their derivatives. They establish a criterion for constructing state transition functions on these polynomials, ensuring uniform mapping of unique results. The unique commutative algebra $\mathbb{K}$ homomorphism connects polynomials to streams, enabling algebraic operations on streams via their polynomial representations. The authors apply this to develop an algebraic geometry decision algorithm for polynomial stream equivalence in the generalized (F, G)-product form and extend it to identify all polynomial equations fitting a user-specified pattern. Florian et al. [31] apply coalgebra to the linguistic semantics of nondeterministic orbit-finite automata and regular nominal nondeterministic automata. They show that the semantics of these automata appear in Kleisli-style coalgebraic tracing semantics and coalgebraic language semantics via generalization. Harsh et al. [32] use module-based logic in coalgebras to describe behavioral equivalence in multi-aspect influence contexts, such as (co)Kleisli categories or Eilenberg-Moore categories. They develop a framework based on indexed categories, demonstrating how coalgebraic behavioral equivalence arises from enhanced relations.

Rutten [33] uses coalgebra as the dual of algebra, focusing on similarity and induction, which lead to two-way simulation and coalgebraic relations. This method formalizes the study of state-based dynamic system behavior. Henning et al. [34] compare four product operators in weighted languages such as convolution, shuffle, infiltration, and Hadamard products demonstrating that weighted languages form an ultimate algebra. They use coinduction to generalize the Newton transform from infinite sequences to weighted languages. Michele [35] observes that the coalgebra of formal exponential series in commutative variables is a final coalgebra within a subclass of coalgebras. A Σ system of partial differential equations under certain conditions leads to an algebraic coalgebra on differential polynomial expressions, enabling an explicit coinductive proof of the existence and uniqueness of solutions to initial value problems. Sprunger [36] develops a correct and complete sequential reasoning system for behavioral equivalence in the coalgebra of a finite set of functions that preserve weak pullback. This mechanism is essential for determining relationships and mappings between structures in coalgebra. Finite functions are examined as they are quotients of polynomial functions, providing built-in signatures and necessary additional axioms.

Rot et al. [37] systematically study bisimulation-up-to techniques to simplify coalgebra methods, enhancing proofs of bisimulations-up-to for various state-based systems like labeled state transition systems, stream systems, and weighted automata. This approach supports compositional reasoning about refinement correctness, simplifying bisimilarity and equivalence proofs. Filippo et al. [38] use mathematical operations semantics with a stream structure to specify operations on infinite sequences of real numbers. They focus on bisimilarity for proving equivalence of closed and open terms, with open terms being equivalent when representing the same stream for all variable instantiations. They introduce bisimulation-up-to substitutions, combining it with bisimulation-up-to techniques to robustly prove open term equivalence.

The equivalence and diversity of symbolic formal languages can be coinductively tested using bisimulation on discriminative automata. Rot et al. [39] introduce simplified bisimulation, providing general conditions for its validity in formal symbolic language operations. They illustrate these results with examples, offering new proofs for classic results like Arden's rule, and cover operators such as union, concatenation, Kleene star, complements, intersections, and shuffle. Joost et al. [40] apply a coalgebraic approach to context-free languages, representing them through systems of behavioral differential equations. They demonstrate new and existing theorems using bisimulation and bisimulation-up-to techniques with linear combinations. Helle et al. [41] study k-regular sequences from a coalgebraic perspective, showing that the set of streams over a semiring S forms a final coalgebra. They characterize k-regular sequences as finite weighted automata, finite systems of behavioral differential equations, and recognizable power series, ultimately achieving this through an isomorphism of the final coalgebra using the k-adic number system. In [42], bisimulation-up-to coalgebra enhances proving bisimulation by allowing some inaccuracy when comparing coalgebraic structures, extending the traditional bisimulation method.

Joost et al. [43] provide three coalgebraic characterizations of context-free languages by adding algebraic structure through pairs of output derivatives. They present a final coalgebraic semantics for interpreting functions into the final coalgebra of all languages with standard output and derivative operations. The first characterization views each derivative as a finite language over non-terminal variables. The second sees derivatives producing elements of an algebraic term. The third adds coalgebraic structure to uniquely closed fixed-point expressions. Marcello et al. [44] present a coinductive definition of context-free power series using behavioral differential equations. They use a coalgebraic approach to unify various algebraic concepts, providing a new proof of the Chomsky and Schützenberger result and showing that the zip operator on two algebraic streams forms an algebra. In [45], the authors apply a coalgebraic perspective to streams for automatic sequences, demonstrating that these sequences form a final coalgebra structure with operators like head, even, and odd. These operators show that automatic sequences relate to general streams as rational languages do to arbitrary languages.

In [46], weighted automata, an extension of nondeterministic automata, include numerical weights for state transitions. Their behavior is expressed as weighted bisimilarity or weighted language equivalence. Coalgebra provides a unified categorical framework for studying state-based systems. The authors show that coalgebra models weighted automata in two ways. First, coalgebras on the category *Set* specify weighted bisimilarity, the category of sets and functions, while coalgebras on the category *Vect*, the category of vector spaces and linear maps, specify weighted language equivalence.

Venanzio [47] applies stream coalgebra in functional programming and type theory, demonstrating the implementation of coinductive types. The study uses corecursion methods to explore general recursion, formal power series, and function tabulation over inductive data, addressing unsafe corecursive equations and non-standard type theory. Joost et al. [48] propose a coalgebraic approach for context-free languages using the functor $\mathfrak{D}(X) = 2 \times X^A$ for deterministic automata over an alphabet A, offering three equivalent characterizations: (1) viewing context-free grammars as $\mathfrak{D}$ coalgebras, (2) defining behavioral differential equations as $\mathfrak{D}$ coalgebras with unique solutions as context-free languages, and (3) interpreting $\mathfrak{D}$ coalgebras as generalized regular expressions with a unique fixed-point operator instead of Kleene star. These provide a foundational basis for defining coalgebraic context-freeness, with semantics defined by the unique homomorphism to the final coalgebra, enabling coinductive proofs of context-free language equivalence.

In [49], the authors discuss that the transformation of a set's structure map into a coalgebra's carrier is not unique. They explore various coalgebraic structures that convert the set of infinite streams into the carrier of a final coalgebra, using cooperators such as head, tail, even, odd, and convolution product. A set of cooperators is complete for a set X if it generates a coalgebraic structure that maps X to a subcoalgebra of the final coalgebra, providing a principle for coalgebraic proof and definition. Silva and Rutten [50] investigate infinite binary trees T_A with nodes labeled in a semiring A from a coalgebraic perspective. They establish principles for coinductive definitions and proofs, noting that T_A has a final coalgebra structure. By viewing these trees as formal power series, the authors create a calculus that presents definitions as behavioral differential equations.

Jiho [51] examines stream algebras and coalgebras, focusing on parameterized properties of families of endofunctors, which can be expressed as parameterized endofunctors. These induce higher-order endofunctors on functor categories, and the study specifies the initial and final coalgebras for these higher-order endofunctors, deriving several results. In [52], the authors present coalgebra as an abstract framework for studying various dynamical systems. An endofunctor F defines both types of F-coalgebra systems and behavioral equivalence among them. Different state-transition systems and their equivalences can be captured by a functor F; for deterministic automata, behavioral equivalence equates to language equivalence, while for nondeterministic automata, it corresponds to ordinary bisimulation. The powerset construction, a standard method for converting nondeterministic automata to equivalent deterministic ones, has been extended to a coalgebraic framework beyond structured state spaces. The authors describe an algebra for polynomial coalgebras of several dynamical systems, including deterministic automata and labeled transition systems, as the coalgebra of polynomial functors constructed from constants and identity relations using product, coproduct, and powerset.

In [53], the authors develop a descriptive language with axiomatization, proving its soundness and completeness via bisimulation through coalgebraic reasoning. They demonstrate the framework's utility by providing a finite system of equations for deterministic and nondeterministic finite automata, explicitly labeled transition systems, and monitored automata over sequences. In [54], the author examines rational streams over a field from a coalgebraic perspective, presenting a unified proof of the equivalence of four representational concepts: finite-dimensional linear systems, finite stream circuits, finite weighted stream automata, and finite-dimensional subsystems of streams. Variants of causal functions on streams are defined, and their interactions are explored from a coalgebraic perspective. In [55], the author shows that the sets of causal and bicausal functions are closed under a certain coinductive structure, which facilitates the construction of new final stream coalgebras over finite alphabets.

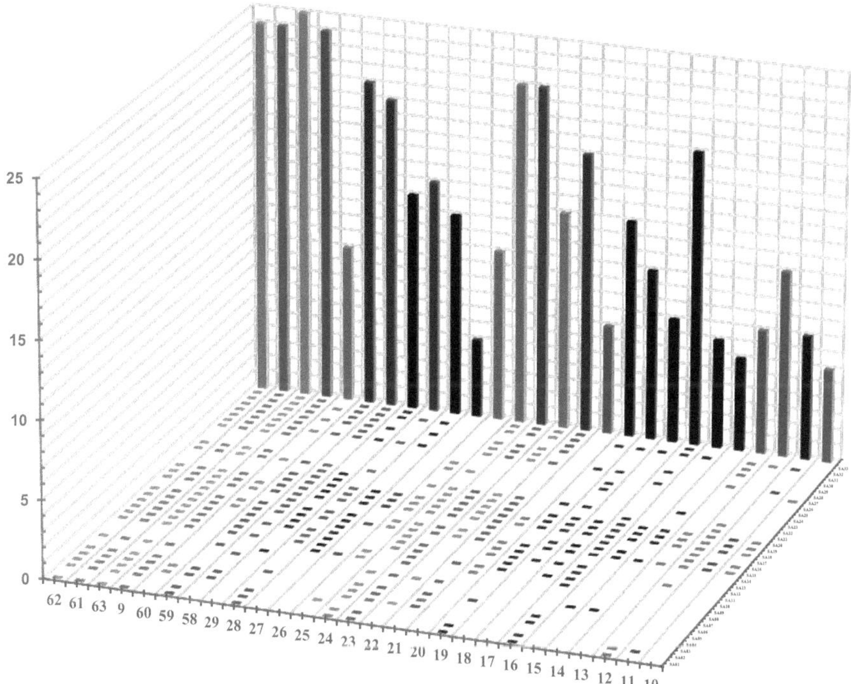

Fig. 2. Representing to contribution of each work on criteria of the stream algebra

In [56], the author introduces the functional stream derivative, generalizing derivatives of rational expressions to stream functions over any input and output alphabets. The construction of Mealy automata from algebraically defined stream functions is demonstrated through symbolic functional stream derivatives, specifically for various bitstream functions in the algebraic calculus of 2-adic numbers. This work aims to model combinational circuits as functions and relations on streams. In [57], the author develops a final coinductive structure for streams, creating a coinductive calculus for infinite real number streams. Central to this is the stream derivative, which supports coinductive proofs and definitions presented as behavioral differential equations. Applications include differential equations, analytical differential equations, continued fractions, and problems from discrete mathematics and combinatorics.

2.3 Comments and New Proposals

Systematizing research on the stream theory, including the stream algebra and stream coalgebra, is most importance as it will encourage and promote researchers in the stream theory to join in big data analytics. This paper analyzes and compares the characteristic criteria of the stream theory that past and current research has contributed through eight analytical and comparative tables, which will be presented in the next subsections. These tables help us envision the future work that we will undertake.

3 Analyzing and Comparing the Stream Theory

3.1 Analyzing the Stream Theory: Applications and Structured Types

The stream theory includes the stream algebra and stream coalgebra. This paper analyzes related work on two characteristic criteria: applications and types of structures. Criterion 1 considers the scope of application of stream theory to the areas of related work. Criterion 2 considers the application of types of data structures of the stream theory in related work. Table 1 and 2 show the analysis of these two criteria as follows.

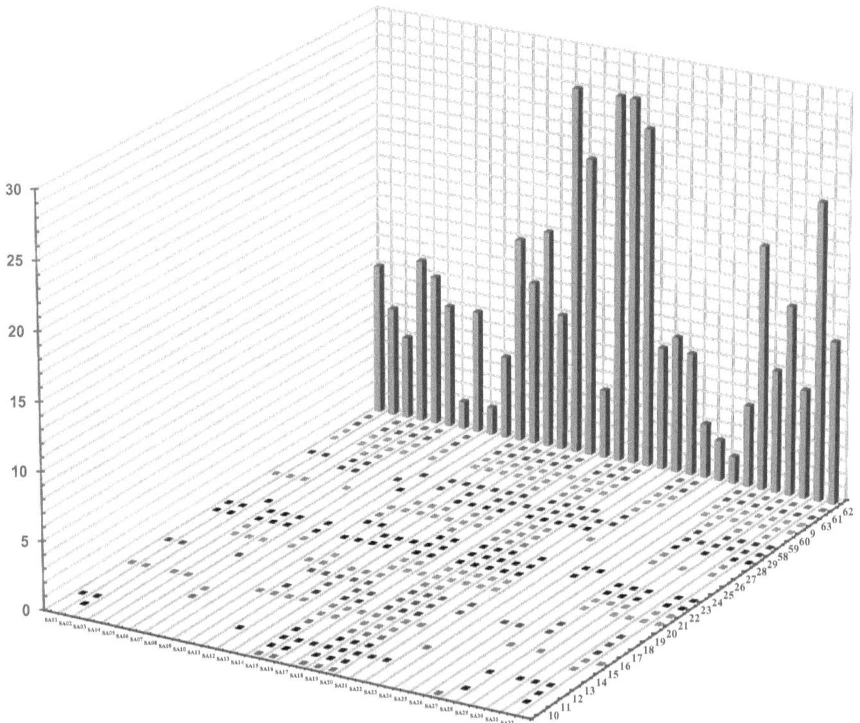

Fig. 3. Representing to contribution of the works with one criterion of the stream algebra

3.2   Analyzing and Comparing the Stream Theory by the Characteristic Criteria

This paper analyzes and compares the stream theory including the stream algebra and the stream coalgebra on the following characteristic criteria. Table 3 gives to analyzing and comparing the stream algebra based on characteristic criteria. Table 4 gives to analyzing and comparing the stream coalgebra based on characteristic criteria.

To easily observe the contribution level of each research work on characteristic criteria, this paper visually represents Table 3 using a multidimensional visual graph in Fig. 2. Meanwhile, the multidimensional visual graph in Fig. 3 shows the contribution levels of the works on individual characteristic criteria. This multidimensional data visualization from a certain perspective based on these characteristic criteria will help researchers understand future development trends of the stream algebra. We apply the nSTM framework proposed by D.V. Pham et al. in 2023 [64] to represent visual graphs in both Fig. 2 and Fig. 3.

Table 1. Analyzing the stream algebra over criteria of applications and structured types

Work	Authors and years	Applications	Structured types
[58]	Kovach et al., 2023	The stream algebra used to compute a contraction expression by using nested streams the authors must choose an attribute ordering and must require that all input streams respect this ordering.	ud
[10]	Helala et al., 2022	The stream algebra is applied to large-scale computer vision systems and its computer vision pipelines.	ud
[59]	Michele et al., 2021	The stream algebra and stream coalgebra used to connections between polynomials, differential equations, and streams.	ud
[60]	Mayuko et al., 2021	Identify a fibrational condition for coincidence between initial algebras and final coalgebras. Identifying algebra and coalgebras in a fiber as inductive and coinductive predicates, coincidence between fibrational initial algebra and final coalgebra allows one to use coinductive witnesses or verifying inductive properties.	ud
[11]	Mauricio et al., 2018	The basic stream operators on the stream algebra that are applied to real and natural number sequence.	ud

(*continued*)

Table 1. (*continued*)

Work	Authors and years	Applications	Structured types
[12]	Helle et al., 2017	The stream differential equations, namely a coinduction method, to specifying streams and stream operators.	ud
[13]	Giorgio et al., 2015	The stream algebra and stream coalgebra to model the syntax and semantics of stochastic processes with multiple continuously occurring states of endogenous functions consistent with the category of unit measure spaces.	ud ssd sd
[14]	Ballester et al., 2015	The algebra and coalgebra duality as a general perspective for studying equations and coequations.	sd ssd ud
[15]	Filippo et al., 2014	Universal algebra and coalgebra to minimize finite automata. This work demonstrates correctness and open up a more general approach.	sd ssd ud
[16]	Niqui and Rutten, 2013	The stream calculus and the stream circuits to define and prove the properties of stream operators as the operators of splitting, partitioning, projecting, and merging data streams.	sd ssd ud
[17]	Kei, 2013	The stream calculus of $1 \perp -$ sequences refer to infinite sequences $\{0, 1, \perp\}$ with almost all copies being at the bottom and is applied in real number calculations within the unit interval $\mathbb{I}$, which is embedded into the stream set $\sum_{\perp,1}^{\omega}$ of sequences. $\{0, 1, \perp\}$.	sd ssd ud
[18]	Ralf, 2011	An alternative solution to induction approach and stream equations that are offered unique solutions. This property gives rise to a fundamental and fascinating proof technique that provides balanced reasoning for the coworld.	sd ssd ud

(continued)

Table 1. (*continued*)

Work	Authors and years	Applications	Structured types
[19]	Kupke et al., 2011	Analyzing the non-standard stream calculus, using different basic operators from the operators of head and tail, to define and argue about streams and stream functions.	sd ssd ud
[20]	Stefan, 2010	To prove the soundness and completeness of the semantic equivalence of finite closed stream circuits, the author relied on prior research that provided a sound and complete calculus for coalgebras for endofunctors on the category of sets.	sd ssd ud
[21]	Marco et al., 2010	The authors are used to stream programming languages and stream rewriting systems to formally represent computational programs on stream data. Currently, no stream calculus has been proposed for such research.	sd ssd ud
[22]	Martin, 2018	The stream programming languages are designed for writing applications that analyze data streams. Data streams or continuous data flows have existed for decades, and the data streams size has increased dramatically. Thus, analyzing large data streams brings tremendous benefits across all current areas.	sd ssd ud
[23]	Milad and Rutten, 2010	The operators of partitioning, projecting, merging, and splitting in stream data programming and stream processing languages.	sd ssd ud
[24]	Vinh and Bowen, 2008	Programming and scheduling of input data stream for a configuration are studied by the authors.	ud

(*continued*)

Table 1. (*continued*)

Work	Authors and years	Applications	Structured types
[25]	Rutten, 2005	A coinductive stream calculus application to signal flow graphs and formal processing to signal flow graphs.	ud
[26]	Rutten, 2005	Analyzing, defining and applying the four different algebraic structures on the bitstreams set that make the foundation for them described as digital circuits.	sd ssd
[27]	Rutten, 2004	Applying the stream algebra includes operators of multiplier, copier, adder, and register to construct signal flow graphs.	sd ssd ud
[28]	Rutten, 2001	Several stream calculus applications are proved as differential equations, analytic differential equations, and continued fractions. A final coalgebraic structure on streams of real numbers and a coinductive calculus on streams are developed.	sd ssd ud
[29]	Tucker et al., 1995	Functional classes proposed to compute on streams over A (The authors say that A is a stream algebra). Parallel computing models are proved to provide the new computational models on the stream algebra over.	sd ssd ud
[61]	Dang Van Pham et al., 2024	The theoretical foundation of some algebraic aspects helps us understand the operating mechanisms of livestream big data. The influence scope of the initiative on the area of big data analytics in the form of livestream.	sd ssd ud
[62]	Dang Van Pham et al., 2024	Verification algorithms and register transfer level specification as algebraic aspects are proposed to verify the register transfer level synthesis results.	sd ssd ud

Notation: sd is structured data, ssd is semi-structured data, and ud is unstructured data.

Table 2. Analyzing the stream coalgebra over criteria of applications and structured types

Work	Authors and years	Applications	Structured types
[30]	Michele et al., 2024	Applying the stream algebra and stream coalgebra to connect polynomials, differential equations, and streams (infinite sequences) over a field $\mathbb{K}$. Construct the (F, G)-products class on streams.	ud
[9]	Dang Van Pham et al., 2023	Apply the stream algebra and stream coalgebra to analytics of big data in livestream.	ud
[63]	Dang Van Pham et al., 2023	Applying the stream algebra and stream coalgebra to analytics of big data in livestream. The authors describe the principle of coinductive approach to verifying synthesis of stream calculus-based computing big data in livestream.	ud
[31]	Florian et al., 2022	Applying the stream coalgebra to the linguistic semantics of the two types including nondeterministic orbit-finite automata and regular nominal nondeterministic automata.	sd ssd ud
[32]	Harsh et al., 2022	Applying module-based logic in stream coalgebras to describe behavioral equivalence in the context of multi-aspect influence.	sd ssd ud
[33]	Rutten, 2019	Applying the coalgebra as a duality of the concept of algebra, this concepts of similarity and induction are two key elements of algebraic theory.	ud
[34]	Henning, 2019	A study comparing of four product operators in weighted languages such as convolution product, shuffle product, infiltration product and hadamard product operators.	sd ssd ud
[35]	Michele, 2019	The coalgebra of formal exponential series in commutative variables is that of the final coalgebra in a subclass of coalgebras.	ud

(continued)

Table 2. (*continued*)

Work	Authors and years	Applications	Structured types
[36]	Sprunger, 2018	A correct and complete sequential reasoning system to reason about the behavioral equivalence of points in the coalgebra of a finite set of functions in preserving weak pullback that is an important type of mechanism to determine the relationships between structures in coalgebra and the mapping between them.	sd ssd ud
[37]	Rot et al., 2017	A systematic study of bisimulation-up-to techniques that simplify methods for coalgebras.	ud
[38]	Filippo et al., 2017	Applying mathematical operator semantics with a stream structure, a specification format for mathematical operators and calculations on streams of real numbers.	sd ssd ud
[39]	Rot et al., 2016	The equivalence and diversity of symbolic formal languages can be tested coinductively by setting up a bisimulation on suitable discriminative automata.	sd ssd ud
[40]	Joost et al., 2015	Providing a coalgebraic approach in terms of the representation of context-free languages, the authors characterized context-free languages as well as power series and stream functions corresponding to context-free languages through systems of behavioral differential equations.	sd ssd ud
[41]	Helle et al., 2014	Studying k-regular sequences from a coalgebraic perspective and building on the observation that the streams set over a semiring S can be viewed as a final coalgebra.	ud
[42]	Rot et al., 2013	Bisimulation-up-to coalgebra that makes it simple coalgebra in analyzing the behavior of coalgebraic structures.	ud

(*continued*)

Table 2. (*continued*)

Work	Authors and years	Applications	Structured types
[43]	Joost et al., 2013	Providing coalgebraic characterizations of the class of context-free languages, each based on the idea of adding algebraic structure to an existing algebraic structure by specifying pairs of output derivatives.	ud
[44]	Marcello et al., 2012	Representing a coinductive definition of context-free power series in terms of behavioral differential equations.	ud
[45]	Kupke et al., 2012	Applying a coalgebraic perspective to streams for automatic sequences.	ud
[46]	Filippo et al., 2012	Coalgebra provides a categorical framework for a unified study of state-based systems and their behaviors.	ud
[47]	Venanzio, 2011	Use the stream coalgebra notions in functional programming and type theory. The stream coalgebra studies general recursion, formal power series on inductive data.	sd ssd ud
[48]	Joost, 2011	A coalgebraic approach for context-free languages by using the functor $\mathfrak{D}(X) = 2 \times X^A$ for deterministic automata over an alphabet A.	sd ssd ud
[49]	Kupke et al., 2010	Different coalgebraic structures that transform the set of infinite streams or sequences into the carrier of a final coalgebra.	sd ssd ud
[50]	Silva et al., 2010	The set of infinite binary trees T_A with nodes labeled in a semiring A from a coalgebraic perspective.	sd ssd ud
[51]	Jiho, 2010	The stream algebras and the stream coalgebras are used to describe the parameterized properties of a family of endofunctors.	sd ssd ud
[52]	Silva et al., 2010	Representing the coalgebra as an abstract framework for the unified research of different types of dynamical systems.	sd ssd ud

(continued)

Table 2. (*continued*)

Work	Authors and years	Applications	Structured types
[53]	Marcello et al., 2009	An algebra for polynomial coalgebras of several dynamical systems, such as deterministic automata and labeled transition systems, is described as the coalgebra of polynomial functors.	ud
[54]	Rutten, 2008	Studying the rational streams over a field from a coalgebraic perspective by exploiting the finiteness of the set of streams.	ud
[55]	Jiho, 2008	Variants of causal functions on streams or on infinite sequences defined and their interactions studied from different perspectives under coalgebraic consideration.	ud
[56]	Rutten, 2006	Representing the concept of the functional stream derivative and generating the notion of derivatives of rational expressions to the case of stream functions over arbitrary input and output alphabets.	ud
[57]	Rutten, 2005	Developing a final coinductive structure on the set of streams to construct a coinductive calculus of streams as sequences of infinite real numbers.	ud

Notation: sd is structured data, ssd is semi-structured data, and ud is unstructured data.

Table 3. Analyzing and comparing the stream algebra by the criteria

No.	Criteria name	[10]	[11]	[12]	[13]	[14]	[15]	[16]	[17]	[18]
SA01	Behavioral differential equations			✓				✓		
SA02	Behavioral sequences of operators		✓	✓				✓		
SA03	Coinductive stream calculus									
SA04	Data stream programming languages							✓		
SA05	Data stream processing languages							✓		
SA06	Head and tail operators on streams									
SA07	Nondeterministic automaton					✓	✓			
SA08	Programs computing on stream data									
SA09	Polynomial streams									
SA10	(Finite) Circuits							✓		

(*continued*)

Table 3. (*continued*)

No.		Description									
SA11		Calculus							✓	✓	
SA12		Differential equations			✓			✓			
SA13		Operators							✓	✓	✓
SA14		Functions									
SA15		Data streams (Finite or Infinite)	✓	✓	✓	✓	✓	✓	✓	✓	✓
SA16		Data sequences	✓	✓	✓			✓	✓	✓	✓
SA17		Dynamic system behavior			✓			✓			
SA18		Formal languages	✓	✓	✓	✓	✓	✓	✓	✓	✓
SA19		Limit or infinite sequences	✓	✓	✓	✓	✓	✓	✓	✓	✓
SA20		Numerical expansions	✓	✓	✓	✓	✓	✓	✓	✓	✓
SA21		Ongoing computations			✓			✓			
SA22		Stream classes			✓						✓
SA23	Data types	Alphabet set A						✓			
SA24		BDL									
SA25		Bitstreams									✓
SA26		Digital streams									✓
SA27		Data streams of image and video	✓						✓		
SA28		Natural number sequences		✓		✓					✓
SA29		Non-rational number sequences							✓		
SA30		Integer number sequences						✓			
SA31		Positive real numbers						✓			
SA32		Real number sequences		✓	✓	✓		✓	✓	✓	✓
SA33		Rational number sequences							✓		

Continue to work

No.	[19]	[20]	[21]	[22]	[23]	[24]	[25]	[26]	[27]	[28]	[29]	[58]	[59]	[60]	[9]	[63]	[61]	[62]
SA01	✓				✓	✓				✓			✓		✓	✓	✓	✓
SA02	✓				✓	✓				✓			✓					
SA03						✓				✓					✓	✓	✓	✓
SA04			✓	✓	✓	✓						✓	✓	✓	✓	✓	✓	✓
SA05			✓		✓	✓						✓	✓	✓	✓	✓	✓	✓
SA06	✓		✓		✓	✓				✓					✓	✓	✓	✓
SA07																		
SA08			✓	✓	✓	✓							✓		✓	✓	✓	✓
SA09											✓		✓					
SA10		✓			✓		✓	✓	✓									
SA11	✓	✓	✓		✓		✓		✓	✓			✓		✓	✓	✓	✓
SA12	✓				✓	✓			✓	✓			✓		✓	✓	✓	✓
SA13	✓	✓			✓	✓			✓	✓	✓	✓	✓		✓	✓	✓	✓
SA14	✓	✓				✓			✓				✓		✓	✓	✓	✓
SA15	✓	✓	✓	✓	✓	✓	✓	✓	✓	✓	✓	✓	✓	✓	✓	✓	✓	✓
SA16		✓	✓	✓	✓	✓			✓	✓	✓	✓	✓	✓	✓	✓	✓	✓
SA17			✓									✓			✓			
SA18	✓	✓	✓	✓	✓	✓	✓	✓	✓	✓	✓	✓	✓	✓	✓	✓	✓	✓
SA19	✓	✓	✓	✓	✓	✓	✓	✓	✓	✓	✓	✓	✓	✓	✓	✓	✓	✓
SA20	✓		✓	✓	✓	✓	✓	✓	✓	✓	✓	✓	✓		✓	✓	✓	✓
SA21			✓	✓	✓	✓					✓	✓	✓					
SA22	✓		✓	✓	✓	✓	✓				✓	✓						
SA23										✓		✓	✓	✓	✓	✓	✓	✓

(*continued*)

Table 3. (*continued*)

SA24															✓	✓	✓	✓
SA25						✓	✓											
SA26							✓											
SA27															✓	✓	✓	✓
SA28	✓		✓	✓	✓	✓			✓	✓	✓	✓	✓	✓	✓	✓	✓	✓
SA29				✓	✓	✓						✓			✓	✓	✓	✓
SA30			✓	✓	✓	✓			✓		✓	✓	✓	✓	✓	✓	✓	✓
SA31			✓									✓	✓		✓	✓	✓	✓
SA32	✓		✓	✓	✓	✓			✓	✓	✓	✓	✓	✓	✓	✓	✓	✓
SA33			✓	✓	✓	✓					✓	✓	✓		✓	✓	✓	✓

Notation: ✓ is contribution.

The analysis in Table 4, based on research by various authors, outlines the key contributions of stream coalgebra. To visualize this better, we used the nSTM framework proposed by D.V. Pham et al. in 2023 [64], visually illustrating the contribution levels of stream coalgebra in both Fig. 4 and Fig. 5.

Table 4. Analyzing and comparing the stream coalgebra by the criteria

Criteria		Work									
No.	Criteria name	[30]	[31]	[32]	[33]	[34]	[35]	[36]	[37]	[38]	[39]
SC01	Behavioral sequences of operators					✓	✓				
SC02	Behavioral differential equations	✓	✓	✓	✓	✓	✓				✓
SC03	Behavioral equivalence										
SC04	Bisimulation: -up-to to coalgebras and relation							✓	✓		
SC05	-up-to techniques and substitutions								✓	✓	✓
SC06	-up-to bisimilarity, reflexivity, and addition								✓		✓
SC07	Classes of functors							✓			
SC08	Coinduction-up-to stream					✓					
SC09	Context-free languages										
SC10	Context-free systems										
SC11	Context-free grammar										
SC12	Context-free streams				✓						
SC13	Coinductive stream calculus	✓			✓	✓					✓

(*continued*)

Table 4. (*continued*)

ID	Category	Concept										
SC14		Class of coalgebras				✓	✓		✓		✓	
SC15		Constant stream X				✓	✓					
SC16		Calculus of bitstreams				✓						
SC17		Deterministic (finite) automata	✓	✓	✓	✓						✓
SC18		Final (stream) coalgebra structure				✓	✓		✓		✓	
SC19		Final system of streams				✓						
SC20		Head and tail operators on streams				✓		✓				
SC21		Infinite or finite streams				✓		✓			✓	
SC22		Linear or dynamical systems				✓						
SC23		Linear stream systems				✓				✓		
SC24		Mealy machines or automata									✓	
SC25		Nondeterministic automaton	✓	✓	✓	✓						✓
SC26		Operators on bitstreams				✓						
SC27		Polynomial streams	✓			✓	✓	✓				
SC28	Streams and stream	Operators				✓	✓	✓				✓
SC29		(Finite) Circuits							✓			
SC30		Calculus	✓			✓	✓		✓	✓	✓	✓
SC31		Differential equations	✓	✓	✓	✓	✓	✓				
SC32		Functions				✓						
SC33		Derivatives	✓				✓					
SC34		Systems				✓					✓	✓
SC35		Behavior				✓						
SC36		Data streams (Finite or Infinite)	✓	✓	✓	✓	✓	✓	✓	✓	✓	✓
SC37		Data sequences	✓	✓	✓	✓	✓	✓	✓	✓	✓	✓
SC38		Dynamic system behavior										
SC39		Formal and streams power series	✓			✓	✓	✓			✓	
SC40		Formal languages	✓	✓	✓	✓	✓	✓	✓	✓	✓	✓
SC41		Limit or infinite sequences	✓	✓	✓	✓	✓	✓	✓	✓	✓	✓
SC42		Numerical expansions				✓						
SC43		Ongoing computations										
SC44		Rational streams				✓	✓					
SC45		Stream classes	✓			✓						
SC46	Weighted	(Linear) Automata				✓		✓		✓		
SC47		Stream automaton				✓						✓
SC48		Language equivalence		✓	✓		✓					
SC49		(Context-free) Languages										
SC50	Data types	Alphabet set A		✓		✓	✓					
SC51		BDL										
SC52		Bitstreams				✓						
SC53		Digital streams										
SC54		Natural number sequences		✓		✓	✓					
SC55		Positive real numbers				✓						
SC56		Real number sequences	✓	✓		✓			✓		✓	

(*continued*)

Table 4. (*continued*)

No.	[40]	[41]	[42]	[43]	[44]	[45]	[46]	[47]	[48]	[49]	[50]	[51]	[52]	[53]	[54]	[55]	[56]	[57]	[59]	[60]	[9]	[63]
SC57	Rational number sequences														✓							
SC58	Integer number sequences												✓	✓	✓							✓

Continue to work

No.	[40]	[41]	[42]	[43]	[44]	[45]	[46]	[47]	[48]	[49]	[50]	[51]	[52]	[53]	[54]	[55]	[56]	[57]	[59]	[60]	[9]	[63]
SC01									✓	✓	✓							✓	✓		✓	✓
SC02	✓	✓			✓				✓	✓	✓							✓	✓		✓	✓
SC03							✓				✓	✓	✓						✓		✓	✓
SC04	✓		✓															✓	✓			
SC05	✓																		✓		✓	✓
SC06			✓		✓														✓			
SC07												✓								✓		
SC08																		✓	✓			
SC09	✓			✓	✓				✓													
SC10	✓				✓				✓													
SC11				✓					✓													
SC12	✓								✓													
SC13	✓										✓											✓
SC14		✓													✓	✓				✓		
SC15															✓						✓	✓
SC16							✓								✓	✓	✓					
SC17		✓		✓					✓				✓	✓								
SC18		✓		✓		✓		✓	✓	✓	✓	✓			✓	✓		✓	✓		✓	✓
SC19										✓						✓					✓	✓
SC20	✓	✓				✓		✓	✓						✓		✓				✓	✓
SC21		✓							✓	✓					✓	✓	✓		✓	✓	✓	✓
SC22													✓	✓	✓							✓
SC23	✓		✓												✓	✓						
SC24													✓		✓		✓	✓				
SC25			✓				✓						✓	✓				✓				
SC26							✓										✓					
SC27	✓					✓									✓			✓				
SC28	✓	✓				✓				✓	✓					✓	✓				✓	✓
SC29															✓	✓	✓				✓	✓
SC30	✓			✓		✓	✓				✓	✓			✓	✓	✓		✓	✓	✓	✓
SC31		✓				✓	✓				✓	✓			✓	✓	✓				✓	✓
SC32					✓						✓	✓			✓	✓					✓	✓
SC33					✓	✓									✓		✓	✓			✓	✓
SC34		✓				✓		✓		✓	✓				✓	✓		✓			✓	✓
SC35										✓	✓				✓	✓		✓			✓	✓
SC36	✓	✓	✓	✓	✓	✓	✓	✓	✓	✓	✓	✓	✓	✓	✓	✓	✓	✓	✓	✓	✓	✓
SC37	✓	✓	✓	✓	✓	✓	✓	✓	✓	✓	✓	✓	✓	✓	✓	✓	✓	✓	✓	✓	✓	✓
SC38													✓	✓							✓	✓
SC39	✓	✓		✓		✓	✓				✓				✓		✓		✓			
SC40	✓	✓	✓	✓	✓	✓	✓	✓	✓	✓	✓	✓	✓	✓	✓	✓	✓	✓	✓	✓	✓	✓
SC41	✓	✓	✓	✓	✓	✓	✓	✓	✓	✓	✓	✓	✓	✓	✓	✓	✓	✓	✓	✓	✓	✓
SC42					✓																	
SC43									✓						✓		✓					
SC44	✓	✓									✓				✓		✓				✓	✓

(continued)

Table 4. (*continued*)

SC45	✓									✓	✓						✓					
SC46	✓	✓				✓							✓		✓			✓				
SC47		✓											✓		✓			✓			✓	✓
SC48													✓									
SC49				✓		✓							✓									
SC50	✓			✓						✓		✓		✓			✓		✓	✓	✓	✓
SC51																			✓		✓	✓
SC52				✓		✓									✓	✓	✓					
SC53				✓											✓	✓	✓					
SC54				✓	✓	✓	✓	✓	✓	✓	✓	✓	✓	✓	✓	✓	✓	✓	✓	✓	✓	✓
SC55	✓									✓											✓	✓
SC56	✓				✓	✓				✓	✓	✓	✓	✓	✓	✓	✓	✓	✓	✓	✓	✓
SC57	✓									✓	✓	✓			✓		✓		✓	✓	✓	✓
SC58	✓			✓		✓				✓	✓	✓	✓	✓		✓	✓	✓	✓	✓	✓	✓

Notation: ✓ is contribution.

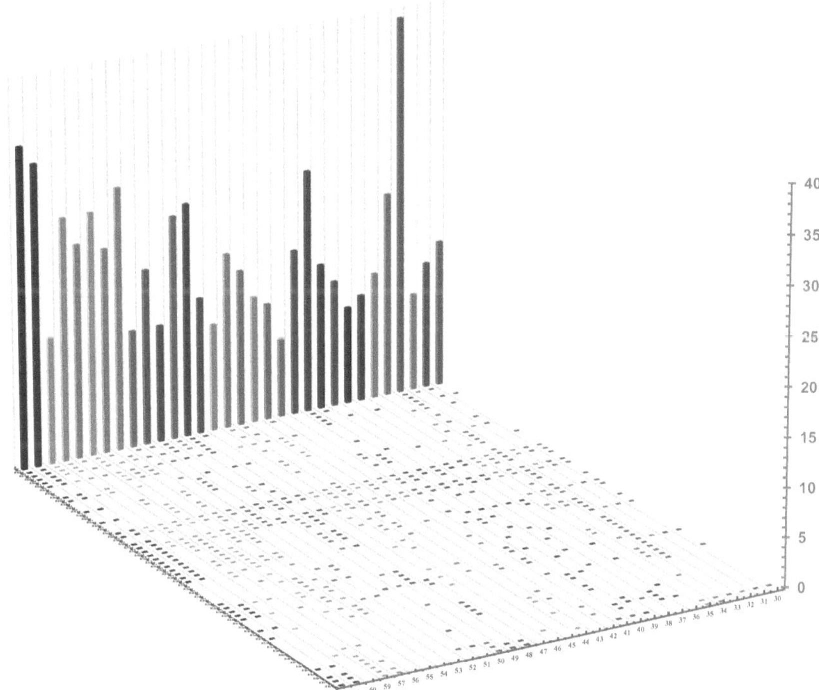

Fig. 4. Representing to contribution of each work on criteria of the stream coalgebra

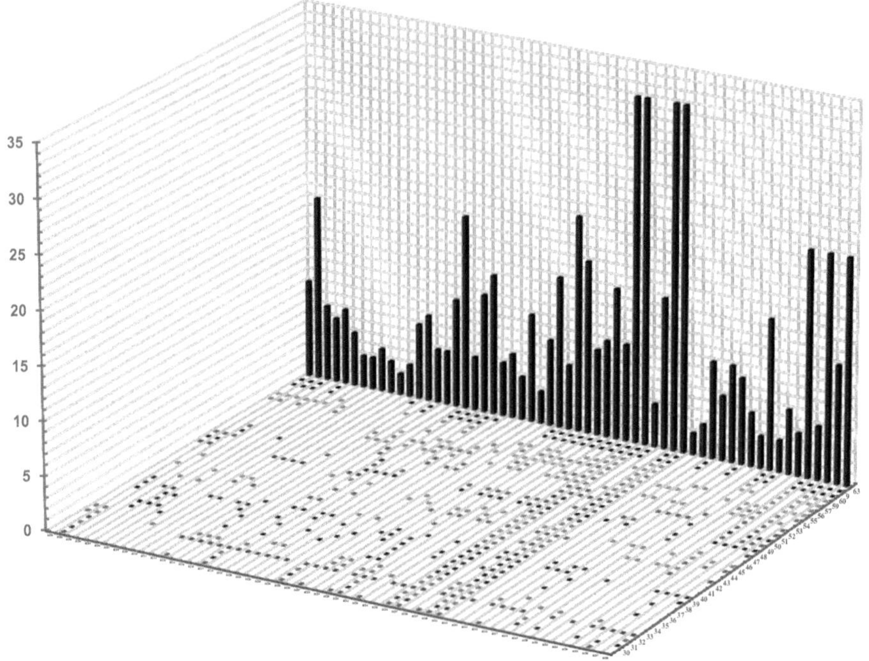

Fig. 5. Representing to contribution of the works with one criterion of the stream coalgebra

3.3   Analyzing and Comparing the Stream Algebra and Coalgebra by Criteria

From the Tables 1, 2, 3 and 4, this paper conducts an analysis and comparison of the similarities and differences of characteristic criteria between the stream algebra and stream coalgebra as contributed by related work from the past to the present (see Tables 5 and 6). This analysis and comparison will provide researchers with a profound understanding of stream theory and offer them a vision to make advancements in the areas of big data analytics and computer science in the future.

3.4   Analyzing and Comparing the Stream Theory by Characteristic Criteria: Extended and Applied Platforms

From Tables 1, 2, 3, 4, 5 and 6, we observe that the analysis and comparison of the stream theory are highly beneficial in big data analytics, enabling us to identify the most characteristic criteria of the contributing stream theory. The related studies have addressed various types of data but have yet to tackle BDL data. Therefore, we have constructed Table 7 to analyze and compare between these related studies and the work conducted by our group using two distinctive criteria. Criterion 1 describes the extended platform of the operators on data streams. Criterion 2 describes the applied platform on the BDL datasets of streams.

Table 5. Analyzing and comparing the stream algebra and coalgebra by the criteria of similarities

Criteria of similarities	Work	
	The stream algebra	The stream coalgebra
Behavioral sequences of operators	[11, 12, 16, 19, 23, 24, 28, 59]	[9, 34, 35, 48–50, 57, 59, 63]
Coinductive stream calculus	[9, 25, 28, 61–63]	[30, 33, 34, 39, 40, 50, 63]
Head and tail operators on streams	[9, 19, 21, 23, 24, 28, 61–63]	[9, 33, 35, 40, 41, 45, 47, 49, 54, 56, 63]
Nondeterministic automaton	[14, 15]	[30–33, 39, 42, 46, 52, 53, 57]
Polynomial streams	[29, 59]	[30, 33–35, 40, 46, 54, 59]
Streams and stream (Finite) circuits	[16, 20, 23, 25–27]	[9, 36, 54–56, 63]
Streams and stream calculus	[9, 16, 17, 19–21, 23, 25, 27, 28, 58, 59, 61–63]	[9, 30, 33, 34, 36–40, 43, 45, 46, 49, 50, 54–57, 59, 63]
Streams and stream differential equations	[9, 12, 16, 19, 23, 24, 27, 28, 59, 61–63]	[9, 30–35, 41, 45, 46, 49, 50, 56, 57, 63]
Streams and stream operators	[9, 16–20, 23, 24, 27–29, 58, 59, 61–63]	[9, 33–35, 39–41, 45, 49, 50, 56, 57, 59, 63]
Stream functions	[9, 19, 20, 24, 27, 29, 59, 61–63]	[9, 33, 47, 49, 50, 56, 57, 63]
Data streams (Finite or Infinite)	[9, 21–29, 58–63]	[9, 30–57, 59, 60, 63]
Data sequences	[9–12, 15–18, 21–25, 27–29, 58–63]	[9, 30–57, 59, 60, 63]
Dynamic system behavior	[12, 16, 21, 58, 63]	[9, 52, 53, 63]
Formal and streams power series	[12]	[30, 33–35, 38, 40, 41, 43, 45, 46, 50, 52, 54–57, 59]
Formal languages	[9–29, 58–63]	[9, 30–57, 59, 60, 63]
Limit or infinite sequences	[9–29, 58–63]	[9, 30–57, 59, 60, 63]
Numerical expansions of stream	[9–29, 58, 59, 61–63]	[33, 45]
Ongoing computations of stream	[12, 16, 21–24, 29, 58, 59]	[49, 54, 56]
Stream classes	[12, 18, 19, 21–25, 29, 58]	[30, 33, 40, 49, 50, 56]

(continued)

Table 5. (*continued*)

Criteria of similarities	Work	
	The stream algebra	**The stream coalgebra**
Alphabet set A	[9, 14, 28, 58–63]	[9, 31, 33, 34, 40, 44, 48, 49, 51, 53, 56, 59, 60, 63]
BDL	[9, 61–63]	[9, 63]
Data streams of image and video	[9, 61–63]	[9, 63]
Bitstreams	[18, 24, 25]	[33, 44, 46, 54–56]
Digital streams	[18, 25]	[44, 54–56]
Natural number sequences	[9, 11, 13, 18, 19, 21–24, 27–29, 58–63]	[9, 31, 33, 34, 43–47, 49–57, 59, 60, 63]
Integer number sequences	[9, 13, 21–24, 27, 29, 58–63]	[9, 31–33, 39, 40, 43, 45, 46, 48–53, 55–57, 59, 60, 63]
Positive real numbers	[9, 13, 21, 58, 59, 61–63]	[9, 33, 40, 49, 63]
Real number sequences	[9, 11–13, 15–19, 21–24, 27–29, 58–63]	[9, 30, 31, 33, 36, 38, 40, 45, 46, 49–57, 59, 60, 63]
Rational number sequences	[9, 16, 21–24, 29, 58, 59, 61–63]	[9, 33, 40, 43, 49–51, 54, 56, 59, 60, 63]

3.5 Analyzing and Comparing the Forms of BDL

BDL is continuously generated in real time by livestream technologies available on social media platforms. Thus, livestream technology is currently considered the most widely used method for supporting various professions, as analyzed and compared in the following Table 8.

Table 6. Analyzing and comparing the stream algebra and coalgebra by the criteria of differences

The stream algebra		The stream coalgebra	
Criteria name	**Work**		**Criteria name**
Data stream programming languages	[9, 16, 21-24, 58-63]	Non	Data stream programming languages
Data stream processing languages	[9, 16, 21, 23, 24, 58-63]	Non	Data stream processing languages
Programs computing on stream data	[21-24, 58] [9, 61-63]	Non	Programs computing on stream data

(*continued*)

Table 6. (*continued*)

The stream algebra			The stream coalgebra
Criteria name	**Work**		**Criteria name**
Data streams of image and video	[10, 16]	*Non*	Data streams of image and video
Non-rational number sequences	[16, 22-24, 58] [9, 61-63]	*Non*	Non-rational number sequences
Behavioral equivalence	*Non*	[9, 46, 50-52, 59, 63]	Behavioral equivalence
Bisimulation-up-to to coalgebras	*Non*	[36, 37, 40, 42, 57, 59]	Bisimulation-up-to to coalgebras, relation
Bisimulation-up-to techniques	*Non*	[37-40, 59]	Bisimulation-up-to techniques, substitutions
Bisimulation-up-to bisimilarity	*Non*	[37, 39, 42, 44, 59]	Bisimulation-up-to bisimilarity, reflexivity, addition
Bisimulation-up-to addition	*Non*	[44]	Bisimulation-up-to addition
Bisimulation-up-to relation	*Non*	[57]	Bisimulation-up-to relation
Classes of functors	*Non*	[36, 51, 60]	Classes of functors
Coinduction-up-to stream	*Non*	[34, 57, 59]	Coinduction-up-to stream
Context-free languages	*Non*	[40, 43, 44, 48]	Context-free languages
Context-free systems	*Non*	[40, 44, 48]	Context-free systems
Context-free grammar	*Non*	[43, 48]	Context-free grammar
Context-free streams	*Non*	[33, 40, 48]	Context-free streams
Class of coalgebras	*Non*	[33, 34, 36, 38, 41, 54, 55]	Class of coalgebras
Constant stream X	*Non*	[9, 33, 34, 54, 63]	Constant stream X
Calculus of bitstreams	*Non*	[33, 47, 54-56]	Calculus of bitstreams
Deterministic (finite) automata	*Non*	[30-33, 39, 41, 43, 48, 52, 53]	Deterministic (finite) automata
Final (stream) coalgebra structure	*Non*	[9, 33, 34, 36, 38, 41, 43, 45, 47-51, 54, 55, 57, 60, 63]	Final (stream) coalgebra structure
Final system of streams	*Non*	[9, 33, 49, 55, 63]	Final system of streams
Linear stream systems	*Non*	[33, 37, 40, 42, 54, 55]	Linear stream systems
Mealy machines or automata	*Non*	[38, 52, 55, 56]	Mealy machines or automata
Operators on bitstreams	*Non*	[33, 47] [56]	Operators on bitstreams
Stream derivatives	*Non*	[30, 34, 45, 46, 54, 56, 57]	Stream derivatives

(*continued*)

Table 6. (continued)

The stream algebra			The stream coalgebra
Criteria name	**Work**		**Criteria name**
Stream system	*Non*	[33, 38, 39, 41, 45, 47, 49, 50, 54, 55, 57]	Stream system
Stream behavior	*Non*	[33, 49, 50, 54, 55, 57]	Stream behavior
Rational streams	*Non*	[33, 34, 40, 41, 50, 54, 56]	Rational streams
Weighted (Linear) automata	*Non*	[33, 35, 37, 40, 41, 46, 52, 54, 57]	Weighted (Linear) automata
Weighted stream automaton	*Non*	[33, 39, 41, 52, 54, 57]	Weighted stream automaton
Weighted language equivalence	*Non*	[31, 32, 34, 46, 52]	Weighted language equivalence
Weighted (Context-free) Languages	*Non*	[44, 46, 52]	Weighted (Context-free) languages

4 Strengths and Shortcomings of the Stream Theory

The stream theory of strengths provides a framework for dealing with streams in a mathematically rigorous way. For formal framework, the stream theory offers a formal mathematical framework to reason about infinite sequences. This rigor is particularly useful in theoretical computer science and formal methods, ensuring that properties and behaviors can be precisely defined and analyzed. Generally, the concepts in the stream theory can be applied across different domains, from computer science to mathematics, providing a unifying approach to dealing with infinite sequences and time varying data.

However, shortcomings of the stream theory of complexity, the formal nature of the stream theory can make it difficult to understand and apply, especially for those not familiar with the underlying mathematical concepts. With abstract nature aspect, the high level of abstraction in the stream theory can sometimes make it challenging to relate to practical problems directly. Bridging the gap between theory and application often requires additional effort. With implementation difficulty aspect, implementing algorithms or systems based on the stream theory can be complex. The theoretical constructs do not always translate easily into efficient computational processes. With limited tool support aspect, comparing to other areas in computer science and mathematics, there is relatively less tool support for working with streams formally. This can make practical experimentation and application more challenging. While the stream theory is very powerful, its application can be quite niche. It is highly relevant in areas requiring formal verification, arithmetical signal processing, and infinite data structures on streams, but may be less applicable to more traditional and finite data problems.

Table 7. Analyzing and comparing between related work and published work of us

Related work			Published work of us			
Work	Authors and years	The operators for general number sequences	Work	Authors and years	Extended platform	Applied platform
[11]	Mauricio et al., 2018	The sequential composition, parallel composition, transformation, synchronized parallel composition, restriction, transformation, reverse, delays, extract, and sum operators on data streams.	[61]	Dang Van Pham et al., 2024	The BDL transformations, automata, combinators for BDL automata.	BDL
[59]	Michele, 2021	The sum and convolution product operators.	[9, 63]	Dang Van Pham et al., 2023	The dropping, taking, zipping, splitting, reverse, merging, (convolution) product, copying, registering, and assignment operators on streams forming BDL	BDL
[16]	Niqui et al., 2013	The splitting, assignment, and merging operators on data streams.				
[27]	Rutten, 2004	The merging and convolution product operators on data streams.				

(*continued*)

Table 7. (*continued*)

Related work			Published work of us			
Work	Authors and years	The operators for general number sequences	Work	Authors and years	Extended platform	Applied platform
[33]	Rutten, 2019	The addition, multiplication, minus, drop, partial sum, Hadamard product, convolution inverse, and splitting stream derivatives operators.				
[34]	Henning et al., 2019	The convolution product, shuffle product, infiltration product, hadamard product, convolution inverse, and shuffle inverse operators				
[35]	Michele, 2019	The sum, product, and partial derivative operators.				
[39]	Rot et al., 2016	The regular operators of union, concatenation and Kleene star as well as language equations with complement and intersection, and shuffle (closure) operators.				

(continued)

Table 7. (*continued*)

Related work			Published work of us			
Work	Authors and years	The operators for general number sequences	Work	Authors and years	Extended platform	Applied platform
[40]	Joost et al., 2015	The zip, even, odd, and unzip operator on streams.				
[41]	Helle et al., 2014	The zip, even, and odd operators on streams.				
[44]	Marcello et al., 2012	The zip operator on streams.				
[45]	Kupke et al., 2012	The head, tail, even, and odd operators on streams.				
[46]	Filippo et al., 2012	The sum, (convolution) product, and inverse operators on streams.				
[47]	Venanzio, 2011	The even, odd, and bind operators on streams.				
[49]	Kupke et al., 2010	The head, tail, even, odd, and convolution product operators on streams.				
[50]	Silva et al., 2010	The head, tail, sum, convolution product, star, and inverse operators on streams.				

(*continued*)

Table 7. (*continued*)

Related work			Published work of us			
Work	Authors and years	The operators for general number sequences	Work	Authors and years	Extended platform	Applied platform
[54]	Rutten, 2008	The head, tail, sum, convolution product, and multiplicative inverse operators on streams.				
[56]	Rutten, 2006	The head, tail, sum, minus, product, and inverse operators on streams.				
[57]	Rutten, 2005	The head, tail, convolution product, shuffle product, shuffle inverse, stream exponentiation, and square root operators on streams.				

4.1 Strengths of the Stream Algebra

The stream algebra is a formal framework for defining and manipulating on streams by using formal algebraic structures. In mathematical foundation area, the stream algebra provides a well-defined and rigorous mathematical framework for reasoning about streams. This accuracy helps ensure the correctness of algorithms and systems that use streams. The stream algebra emphasizes the composition of operators, allowing complex streams to be built from simpler ones. This compositional nature aids in modularity and reuse of components. With expressiveness, the algebraic approach allows for the definition of a wide range of operators on streams, including arithmetic operators and transformations on streams. This makes the stream algebra highly expressive and flexible. In addition, the stream algebra often leads to declarative descriptions of stream operators, making it easier to specify what should be done rather than how it should be done. This can simplify reasoning and verification. The stream algebra is inherently designed to handle infinite sequences, making it suitable for applications involving continuous data streams, such as signal processing, real-time systems, and reactive programming.

In modularity and composition, the stream algebra allows for the modular composition of streams. This means complex streams can be built up from simpler components,

Table 8. Analyzing and comparing types of professions using the livestream technology

Work	Years	The forms of BDL	BDL
[65–68]	2018 2019 2021 2022	Livestream in merchandizing	Data viewed and purchased from users' online shopping. Online shopping data helps identify factors that influence purchase intent, providing a convenient, flexible shopping experience that makes interactions faster and more entertaining. Serves as a basis for improving satisfaction and helping to increase consumers' intention to continuously use online shopping.
[69]	2022	Livestream in traveling	Tour destination data streamed online by livestream technology will always have the characteristics of immediacy, realistic and lively interaction, creating a form that positively influences the feeling of presence and trust of consumers, and enhances and directly influences customers' travel intention.
[70]	2021	Livestream in healthcare	Surgical data is streamed in real time by livestream technology through a livestream from the surgical simulator, images are transferred from a digital surgical microscope and an environmental camera at high quality. High resolution will help students grasp surgical techniques clearly and accurately.
[70, 71]	2020 2021	Livestream in education	Lecture data is streamed online through livestream technology. Lecture data is organized by lecturers to create optional workflows with interactive activities between lecturers and students including polls, questions and answers, instant feedback, and interactive group creation.

facilitating both understanding and construction. With expressiveness, the stream algebra can describe a wide variety of operators on streams, making it a versatile tool for both practical applications like signal processing and theoretical explorations like formal language theory.

4.2   Shortcomings of the Stream Algebra

The high level of abstraction in the stream algebra can make it challenging for practitioners who are not familiar with advanced mathematical concepts. This can limit its accessibility and practical use. Translating algebraic specifications into efficient and effective implementations can be difficult. The theoretical constructs do not always map directly to practical and performant code. There is relatively limited tool support for the stream algebra compared to more mainstream programming paradigms. This can hinder its adoption and make practical experimentation more challenging. The formalism and notation used in the stream algebra can be difficult to learn for those without a strong background in mathematics or formal methods. The stream algebra is particularly useful in specific domains that deal with infinite or continuous data streams, such as signal processing, formal verification, and reactive systems. However, its applicability to more conventional, finite data problems is limited. While the stream algebra provides a clear and formal way to describe operators on streams, ensuring that these operators are performed efficiently, especially in real-time or resource-constrained environments, can be challenging.

4.3   Strengths of the Stream Coalgebra

The stream coalgebra is a mathematical framework that provides a coinductive approach to defining and reasoning about streams. The stream coalgebra leverages coinduction, a powerful method for reasoning about infinite structures. This is particularly useful for defining and proving properties of streams that are inherently infinite. The coalgebraic methods focus on the behavior of systems over time, making them well-suited for modeling dynamic and evolving systems. This is beneficial in areas like reactive systems, where the state changes continuously. Like the stream algebra, the stream coalgebra supports the modular construction of streams. Complex behaviors can be described by composing simpler coalgebraic structures, promoting reuse and clarity. The stream coalgebra provides a highly expressive framework for defining a wide variety of operators and transformations on streams. This flexibility is valuable in both theoretical and practical applications. Especially duality with algebra, the duality between the stream algebra and stream coalgebra provides a rich interaction of concepts and techniques, offering deeper insights and alternative approaches to problems involving infinite data structures. There are specialized tools and frameworks that support coinductive reasoning, which can aid in formal verification and proof of properties for systems modeled using the stream coalgebra. In coinduction, the use of coinduction in the stream coalgebra is a powerful method for defining and reasoning about streams. Coinduction is particularly useful for proving properties of infinite structures, which would be cumbersome or impossible with induction alone.

4.4   Shortcomings of the Stream Coalgebra

The coinductive nature and the abstract mathematical concepts involved in the stream coalgebra can be difficult to grasp, especially for those without a strong background in theoretical computer science or mathematics. Translating the stream coalgebraic specifications into efficient, real-world implementations can be challenging. The abstract nature of coalgebra doesn't always map easily to practical programming paradigms. While there are tools for coinduction, the overall ecosystem of tools and libraries for the stream coalgebra is less developed compared to more mainstream programming approaches. This can hinder practical adoption and experimentation. The stream coalgebra is particularly well-suited for modeling systems with infinite or ongoing behaviors, such as reactive systems, formal verification, and certain types of data streams. However, its applicability to more conventional, finite data problems is limited. The formalism and notation used in the stream coalgebra can be difficult to learn, requiring a strong understanding of coinduction and related mathematical concepts. Ensuring that stream coalgebraic models and operators perform efficiently, especially in resource limited environments or real time applications, can be challenging. The abstract nature of coalgebra may lead to less straightforward optimization strategies.

4.5 Applying the Platforms of the Stream Theory in Computing BDL

The stream theory in the context of big data in generally and BDL in particularly revolves around the processing of data streams in real-time. Applying the platforms of stream theory to computing BDL involves several key principles and technologies designed to handle continuous data flow efficiently. The main platforms and approaches are used to a distributed streaming platform that allows the building of real-time data pipelines and streaming applications. Apache Kafka is used for high-throughput and low-latency data streams. A stream processing framework with powerful capabilities for stateful computations over infinite and finite data streams. Apache Flink is known for its low latency and high throughput. A real-time computation system of Apache Storm that makes it easy to process infinite data streams of data reliably [9, 72–89]. By combining these platforms and techniques, we can build a robust and efficient system for computing and analyzing BDL, providing real-time insights and enhancing the overall live streaming experience.

5 Discussions

The stream theory, with it is the stream algebra and the coalgebra components, is a robust and flexible framework for dealing with data streams or infinite data sequences. Its strengths lie in its formal rigor, modularity, and powerful coinductive reasoning. However, it also faces challenges in terms of complexity, abstraction, implementation difficulty, limited tool support, and niche applications. For those working within its scope, it offers powerful tools, but its adoption may be limited by the above mentioned shortcomings.

The stream algebra offers a powerful and expressive framework for working with infinite data sequences, with strengths in its mathematical rigor, compositionality, and suitability for continuous data. However, its high level of abstraction, complexity in implementation, limited tool support, and potential efficiency concerns are significant shortcomings that can limit its practical applicability and adoption.

The stream coalgebra provides a powerful and expressive framework for dealing with streams, with strengths in coinductive reasoning, behavioral semantics, modularity, and the duality with algebra. However, its complexity, abstraction, implementation challenges, limited tooling, and specialized use cases are significant shortcomings that can limit its practical application and broader adoption. For those working within its scope, it offers robust tools for modeling and reasoning about infinite behaviors, but it requires a solid theoretical foundation to use effectively.

6 Conclusions and Future Work

This paper systematized related research and presents analytical and comparative tables based on the characteristic criteria contributed by stream theory. Through detailed analysis, it offers researchers insights into various data types, structured types, and operating systems. This paper includes eight tables that analyze and compare related research works, highlighting how the stream theory has influenced big data analytics, particularly in live streaming contexts. These tables provide researchers with a comprehensive overview of stream theory, encompassing both stream algebra and stream coalgebra, from past to present. This foundational theory is crucial for envisioning future research and serves as a vital framework for developing data science analytical systems and new formal theoretical platforms. Our team's next research direction will be to apply stream theory to analyze and develop stream theory for big data in the form of livestreams, and to integrate it with algebraic structures (such as monoid structures) in the computation of big data for livestreams in particularly and big data in generally.

References

1. Vijesh Joe, C., Raj, J.S., Smys, S.: Big data analytics: tools, challenges, and scope in data-driven computing. In: Raj, J.S. (eds,) ICMCSI 2020, pp. 709–719. Springer, Cham (2021). https://doi.org/10.1007/978-3-030-49795-8_67
2. Vashisht, P., Gupta, V.: Big data analytics techniques: a survey. In: International Conference on Green Computing and Internet of Things (ICGCIoT), pp. 264–269 (2015). https://doi.org/10.1109/ICGCIoT.2015.7380470
3. Taleb, I., Serhani, M.A., Dssouli, R.: Big data quality assessment model for unstructured data. In: International Conference on Innovations in Information Technology (IIT), Al Ain, United Arab Emirates, pp. 69–74. IEEE (2019). https://doi.org/10.1109/Innovations.2018.8605945
4. Stefanowski, J., Krawiec, K., Wrembel, R.: Exploring complex and big data. Int. J. Appl. Math. Comput. Sci. **27**(4), 669–679 (2017). https://doi.org/10.1515/amcs-2017-0046
5. V.S and S. S, "Research in Big Data - An Overview," *Informatics Engineering, an International Journal,* vol. 4, no. 3, pp. 01–20, 2016, https://doi.org/10.5121/ieij.2016.4301
6. Rajaraman, V.: Big data analytics. Resonance **21**(8), 695–716 (2016). https://doi.org/10.1007/s12045-016-0376-7
7. Gandomi, A., Haider, M.: Beyond the hype: Big data concepts, methods, and analytics. Int. J. Inf. Manage. **35**(2), 137–144 (2015). https://doi.org/10.1016/j.ijinfomgt.2014.10.007
8. Naeem, M., et al.: Trends and future perspective challenges in big data. In: Pan, J.-S., Balas, V.E., Chen, C.-M. (eds.) Advances in Intelligent Data Analysis and Applications 2022, pp. 309–325. Springer, Singapore (2022). ISBN: 978-981-16-5036-9, https://doi.org/10.1007/978-981-16-5036-9_30

9. Pham, D.V., Phan, V.C.: Overview of the stream theory-based big data in livestream. J. Mob. Networks Appl. 1–14 (2023). https://doi.org/10.1007/s11036-023-02180-0, ISSN: 1572–8153

10. Helala, M.A., Qureshi, F.Z., Pu, K.Q.: A stream algebra for performance optimization of large scale computer vision pipelines. IEEE Trans. Pattern Anal. Mach. Intell. **44**(2), 905–923 (2022). https://doi.org/10.1109/TPAMI.2020.3015867

11. Toro, M., Desainte-Catherine, M., Janin, D., Orlarey, Y.: Real-time interactive streams and temporal objects language. Osfpreprints (2018). https://doi.org/10.31219/osf.io/a6stk

12. Hansen, H.H., Kupke, C., Rutten, J.J.M.M.: Stream differential equations: specification formats and solution methods. Log. Methods Comput. Sci. **13**(1) (2017). https://doi.org/10.23638/LMCS-13(1:3)2017

13. Bacci, G., Miculan, M.: Structural operational semantics for continuous state stochastic transition systems. J. Comput. Syst. Sci. **81**(5), 834–858 (2015). https://doi.org/10.1016/j.jcss.2014.12.003

14. Ballester-Bolinches, A., Cosme-Llópez, E., Rutten, J.: The dual equivalence of equations and coequations for automata. Inf. Comput. **244**(C), 49–75 (2015). https://doi.org/10.1016/j.ic.2015.08.001

15. Bonchi, F., Bonsangue, M.M., Hansen, H.H., Panangaden, P., Rutten, J.J.M.M., Silva, A.: Algebra-coalgebra duality in Brzozowski's minimization algorithm. ACM Trans. Comput. Logic **15**(1), 1–29 (2014). https://doi.org/10.1145/2490818

16. Niqui, M., Rutten, J.J.M.M.: Stream processing coalgebraically. Sci. Comput. Program. **78**(11), 2192–2215 (2013). https://doi.org/10.1016/j.scico.2012.07.013

17. Terayama, K., Tsuiki, H.: A stream calculus of bottomed sequences for real number computation. Electron. Not. Theor. Comput. Sci. **298**, 383–402 (2013). https://doi.org/10.1016/j.entcs.2013.09.023

18. Hinze, R.: Concrete stream calculus: an extended study. J. Funct. Program. **20**(5–6), 463–535 (2011). https://doi.org/10.1017/S0956796810000213

19. Kupke, C., Niqui, M., Rutten, J.: Stream differential equations: concrete formats for coinductive definitions. Oxford University, Technical report No.RR-11–10, 2011 (2011)

20. Milius, S.: A sound and complete calculus for finite stream circuits. In: Proceedings of the Annual IEEE Symposium on Logic in Computer Science, pp. 421–430. IEEE Computer Society (2010). https://doi.org/10.1109/lics.2010.11

21. Gaboardi, M., Saurin, A.: A foundational calculus for computing with streams. In: 12th Italian Conference on Theoretical Computer Science (2010)

22. Hirzel, M., Baudart, G., Bonifati, A., Valle, E.D., Sakr, S., Vlachou, A.A.: Stream processing languages in the big data era. SIGMOD Rec. **47**(2), 29–40 (2018). https://doi.org/10.1145/3299887.3299892

23. Niqui, M., Rutten, J.: Sampling, splitting and merging in coinductive stream calculus. In: Bolduc, C., Desharnais, J., Ktari, B. (eds.) Mathematics of Program Construction. vol. 6120, pp. 310–330. Springer, Heidelberg (2010). https://doi.org/10.1007/978-3-642-13321-3_18

24. Vinh, P.C., Bowen, J.P.: Formalization of data flow computing and a coinductive approach to verifying flowware synthesis. In: Gavrilova, M.L., Tan, C.J.K. (eds.) Transactions on Computational Science I. LNCS, vol. 4750, pp. 1–36. Springer, Heidelberg (2008). https://doi.org/10.1007/978-3-540-79299-4_1

25. Rutten, J.J.M.M.: A tutorial on coinductive stream calculus and signal flow graphs. Theoret. Comput. Sci. **343**(3), 443–481 (2005). https://doi.org/10.1016/j.tcs.2005.06.019

26. Rutten, J.: Algebra, bitstreams, and circuits. CWI, Technical report SEN-R0502, vol. 16 (2005). ISSN: 1386–369X

27. Rutten, J.J.M.M.: An application of stream calculus to signal flow graphs. In: de Boer, F.S., Bonsangue, M.M., Graf, S., de Roever, W.-P. (eds.) Formal Methods for Components

and Objects, pp. 276–291. Springer, Heidelberg (2004). https://doi.org/10.1007/978-3-540-30101-1_13

28. Rutten, J.J.M.M.: Elements of stream calculus (an extensive exercise in coinduction). Electron. Not. Theoret. Comput. Sci. **45**, 358–423 (2001). https://doi.org/10.1016/S1571-0661(04)809 72-1. CWI (Centre for Mathematics and Computer Science), Published by Elsevier Science B. V

29. Tucker, J.V., Zucker, J.I.: Computable functions on stream algebras. In: Schwichtenberg, H. (ed.) Proof and Computation, vol. 139 pp. 397–437. Springer, Heidelberg (1995). ISBN: 978-3-642-79361-5, https://doi.org/10.1007/978-3-642-79361-5_10

30. Boreale, M., Collodi, L., Gorla, D.: Products, polynomials and differential equations in the stream calculus. ACM Trans. Comput. Logic **25**(1), 1–26 (2024). ISSN: 1529–3785, https://doi.org/10.1145/3632747

31. Frank, F., Milius, S., Urbat, H.: Coalgebraic semantics for nominal automata. In: Cham, Hansen, H.H., Zanasi, F. (eds.) Coalgebraic Methods in Computer Science. LNCS, vol. 13225, pp. 45–66. Springer, Cham (2022). https://doi.org/10.1007/978-3-031-10736-8_3

32. Beohar, H., König, B., Küpper, S., Mika-Michalski, C.: Predicate and relation liftings for coalgebras with side effects: an application in coalgebraic modal logic. In: Hansen, H.H., Zanasi, F. (eds.) CMCS 2022. LNCS, vol. 13225, pp. 1–22. Springer, Cham (2022). https://doi.org/10.1007/978-3-031-10736-8_1

33. Rutten, J.: The Method of Coalgebra: Exercises in Coinduction, p. 261. CWI, The Netherlands (2019). ISBN: 978-90-6196-568-8

34. Basold, H., Hansen, H.H., Pin, J.-E., Rutten, J.: Newton series, coinductively: a comparative study of composition. In: Mathematical Structures in Computer Science, pp. 1–29. (2019). https://doi.org/10.1017/S0960129517000159

35. Boreale, M.: On the coalgebra of partial differential equations. In: 44th International Symposium on Mathematical Foundations of Computer Science (MFCS 2019), vol. 138, in Leibniz International Proceedings in Informatics (LIPIcs), pp. 1–24 (2019). https://doi.org/10.4230/LIPIcs.MFCS.2019.24

36. Sprunger, D.: A complete logic for behavioural equivalence in coalgebras of finitary set functors. J. Log. Algebr. Methods Program. **94**, 184–199 (2018). https://doi.org/10.1016/j.jlamp.2017.05.001

37. Rot, J., Bonchi, F., Bonsangue, M., Pous, D., Rutten, J.A.N., Silva, A.: Enhanced coalgebraic bisimulation. Math. Struct. Comput. Sci. **27**(7), 1236–1264 (2017). https://doi.org/10.1017/S0960129515000523

38. Bonchi, F., Lee, M.D., Rot, J.: Bisimilarity of open terms in stream GSOS. In: Dastani, M., Sirjani, M. (eds.) Fundamentals of Software Engineering, pp. 35–50. Springer, Cham (2017). ISBN: 978-3-319-68972-2, https://doi.org/10.1007/978-3-319-68972-2_3

39. Rot, J., Bonsangue, M., Rutten, J.: Proving language inclusion and equivalence by coinduction, Inf. Comput. **246**, 62–76 (2016). ISSN: 0890–5401, https://doi.org/10.1016/j.ic.2015.11.009

40. Winter, J., Bonsangue, M.M., Rutten, J.J.M.M.: Context-free coalgebras. J. Comput. Syst. Sci. **81**(5), 911–939 (2015). ISSN: 0022–0000, https://doi.org/10.1016/j.jcss.2014.12.004

41. Hansen, H.H., Kupke, C., Rutten, J., Winter, J.: A final coalgebra for k-regular sequences. In: van Breugel, F., Kashefi, E., Palamidessi, C., Rutten, J. (eds.) Horizons of the Mind. A Tribute to Prakash Panangaden: Essays Dedicated to Prakash Panangaden on the Occasion of His 60th Birthday, pp. 363–383. Springer, Cham (2014). ISBN: 978-3-319-06880-0. https://doi.org/10.1007/978-3-319-06880-0_19

42. Rot, J., Bonsangue, M., Rutten, J.: Coalgebraic bisimulation-up-to. In: van Emde Boas, P., Groen, F.C.A., Italiano, G.F., Nawrocki, J., Sack, H. (eds.) SOFSEM 2013: Theory and Practice of Computer Science 2013, vol. 7741, pp. 369–381. Springer, Heidelberg (2013). ISBN: 978-3-642-35843-2. https://doi.org/10.1007/978-3-642-35843-2_32

43. Winter, J., Rutten, J.J.M., Bonsangue, M.M.: Coalgebraic characterizations of context-free languages. Log. Meth. Comput. Sci. **9**(3) (2013). https://doi.org/10.2168/lmcs-9(3:14)2013
44. Bonsangue, M.M., Rutten, J., Winter, J.: Defining context-free power series coalgebraically. In: Pattinson, D., Schröder, L. (eds.) Coalgebraic Methods in Computer Science, pp. 20–39. Springer, Heidelberg (2012). https://doi.org/10.1007/978-3-642-32784-1_2
45. Kupke, C., Rutten, J.J.M.M.: On the final coalgebra of automatic sequences. In: Constable, R.L., Silva, A. (eds.) Logic and Program Semantics: Essays Dedicated to Dexter Kozen on the Occasion of His 60th Birthday, pp. 149–164. Springer, Heidelberg (2012). ISBN: 978–3-642-29485-3. https://doi.org/10.1007/978-3-642-29485-3_10
46. Bonchi, F., Bonsangue, M., Boreale, M., Rutten, J., Silva, A.: A coalgebraic perspective on linear weighted automata. Inf. Comput. **211**, 77–105 (2012). ISSN: 0890-5401. https://doi.org/10.1016/j.ic.2011.12.002
47. Capretta, V.: Coalgebras in functional programming and type theory. Theoret. Comput. Sci. **412**(38), 5006–5024 (2011). https://doi.org/10.1016/j.tcs.2011.04.024
48. Winter, J., Bonsangue, M.M., Rutten, J.: Context-free languages, coalgebraically. In: Corradini, A., Klin, B., Cîrstea, C. (eds.) Algebra and Coalgebra in Computer Science, vol. 6859, pp. 359–376. Springer, Heidelberg (2011). ISBN: 978-3-642-22944-2. https://doi.org/10.1007/978-3-642-22944-2_25
49. Kupke, C., Rutten, J.: Complete sets of cooperations. Inf. Comput. **208**(12), 1398–1420 (2010). ISSN: 0890-5401. https://doi.org/10.1016/j.ic.2009.10.009
50. Silva, A., Rutten, J.: A coinductive calculus of binary trees. Inf. Comput. **208**(5), 578–593 (2010). https://doi.org/10.1016/j.ic.2008.08.006
51. Kim, J.: Higher-order algebras and coalgebras from parameterized endofunctors. Electron. Not. Theoret. Comput. Sci. **264**(2), 141–154 (2010). https://doi.org/10.1016/j.entcs.2010.07.018
52. Silva, A., Bonchi, F., Bonsangue, M.M., Rutten, J.J.M.M.: Generalizing the powerset construction, coalgebraically. In: IARCS Annual Conference on Foundations of Software Technology and Theoretical Computer Science (FSTTCS), vol. 8, in Leibniz International Proceedings in Informatics (LIPIcs), pp. 272–283 (2010). https://doi.org/10.4230/LIPIcs.FSTTCS.2010.272
53. Bonsangue, M., Rutten, J., Silva, A.: An algebra for Kripke polynomial coalgebras. In: 2009 24th Annual IEEE Symposium on Logic in Computer Science, pp. 49–58 (2009). https://doi.org/10.1109/LICS.2009.18
54. Rutten, J.: Rational streams coalgebraically. Logical Meth. Comput. Sci. **4**(3:9), 1–22 (2008). https://doi.org/10.2168/LMCS-4(3:9)2008
55. Kim, J.: Coinductive properties of causal maps. In: Meseguer, J., Roşu, G. (eds.) Algebraic Methodology and Software Technology, pp. 253–267. Springer, Heidelberg (2008). https://doi.org/10.1007/978-3-540-79980-1_20
56. Rutten, J.J.M.M.: Algebraic specification and coalgebraic synthesis of mealy automata. Electronic Not. Theor. Comput. Sci. **160**, 305–319 (2006). https://doi.org/10.1016/j.entcs.2006.05.030
57. Rutten, J.J.M.M.: A coinductive calculus of streams. Math. Struct. Comput. Sci. **15**(1), 93–147 (2005). https://doi.org/10.1017/S0960129504004517. Association for Computing Machinery, Cambridge University Press United States
58. Kovach, S., Kolichala, P., Gu, T., Kjolstad, F.: Indexed streams: a formal intermediate representation for fused contraction programs. In: Proceedings of the ACM on Programming Languages, vol. 7, no. PLDI, pp. 1169–1193 (2023). https://doi.org/10.1145/3591268
59. Boreale, M., Gorla, D.: Algebra and coalgebra of stream products. In: 32nd International Conference on Concurrency Theory (CONCUR 2021). Leibniz International Proceedings in Informatics (LIPIcs), vol. 203: Schloss Dagstuhl – Leibniz-Zentrum für Informatik, pp. 19:1–19:17 (2021). https://doi.org/10.4230/LIPIcs.CONCUR.2021.19

60. Kori, M., Hasuo, I., Katsumata, S.-Y.: Fibrational initial algebra-final coalgebra coincidence over initial algebras: turning verification witnesses upside down. In: 32nd International Conference on Concurrency Theory (CONCUR 2021). Leibniz International Proceedings in Informatics (LIPIcs), vol. 203: Schloss Dagstuhl – Leibniz-Zentrum für Informatik, pp. 21:1–21:22 (2021). https://doi.org/10.4230/LIPIcs.CONCUR.2021.21

61. Pham, D.V., Phan, V.C.: Algebraic aspects of big data in livestream in internet of mobile things. J. Mob. Networks Appl. (2024). ISSN: 1572-8153. https://doi.org/10.1007/s11036-024-02297-w

62. Van Pham, D., Phan, V.C., Nguyen, B.K.: Algebraic semantics of register transfer level in synthesis of stream calculus-based computing big data in Livestream. In: Cong Vinh, P., Mahfooz Ul Haque, H. (eds.) EAI ICTCC 2023. LNICST, vol. 586, pp. 19–35., Springer, Cham (2024). ISSN: 1867–8211. https://doi.org/10.1007/978-3-031-59462-5_2

63. Van Pham, D., Phan, V.C., Nguyen, B.K.: Formally specifying and coinductive approach to verifying synthesis of stream calculus-based computing big data in Livestream. Internet of Things **23**, 100878 (2023). https://doi.org/10.1016/j.iot.2023.100878

64. Pham, D.V., Nguyen, B.K.: A visual analytics approach applying for discovering knowledge from multivariate datasets of stakeholders feedback in the university. Vietnam J. Comput. Sci. **10**(04), 463–483 (2023). https://doi.org/10.1142/S2196888823500082

65. Liu, X., Kim, S.H.: Beyond shopping: the motivations and experience of live stream shopping viewers. In: 2021 13th International Conference on Quality of Multimedia Experience (QoMEX), pp. 187–192 (2021). https://doi.org/10.1109/QoMEX51781.2021.9465387

66. Chen, L.Y.: The effects of livestream shopping on customer satisfaction and continuous purchase intention. Int. J. Adv. Stud. Comput. Sci. Eng. **8**(4), 1–9 (2019). in English

67. Doanh, N.K., Do Dinh, L., Quynh, N.N.: Tea farmers' intention to participate in Livestream sales in Vietnam: the combination of the technology acceptance model (TAM) and barrier factors. J. Rural Stud. **94**, 408–417 (2022). https://doi.org/10.1016/j.jrurstud.2022.05.023

68. Cai, J., Wohn, D.Y., Mittal, A., Sureshbabu, D.: Utilitarian and hedonic motivations for live streaming shopping. In: Presented at the proceedings of the ACM international conference on interactive experiences for TV and online video, SEOUL, Republic of Korea (2018). https://doi.org/10.1145/3210825.3210837

69. Zheng, S., Wu, M., Liao, J.: The impact of destination live streaming on viewers' travel intention. Current Issues Tourism 1–15 (2022). https://doi.org/10.1080/13683500.2022.2117594

70. van Bonn, S.M., Grajek, J.S., Schneider, A., Oberhoffner, T., Mlynski, R., Weiss, N.M.: Interactive live-stream surgery contributes to surgical education in the context of contact restrictions. Eur Arch Otorhinolaryngol. (2021). https://doi.org/10.1007/s00405-021-06994-0

71. Kubica, T., Hara, T., Braun, I., Schill, A.: An approach to support interactive activities in live stream lectures. In: Addressing Global Challenges and Quality Education, vol. 12315, pp. 432–436. Springer, Cham (2020). https://doi.org/10.1007/978-3-030-57717-9_40

72. Ashabi, A., Sahibuddin, S.B., Haghighi, M.S.: Big data: current challenges and future scope. In: IEEE 10th Symposium on Computer Applications & Industrial Electronics (ISCAIE), pp. 131–134 (2020). https://doi.org/10.1109/ISCAIE47305.2020.9108826

73. Vassakis, K., Petrakis, E., Kopanakis, I.: Big data analytics: applications, prospects and challenges. In: Skourletopoulos, G., Mastorakis, G., Mavromoustakis, C., Dobre, C., Pallis, E. (eds.) Mobile Big Data: A Roadmap from Models to Technologies, pp. 3–20. Springer, Cham (2018). https://doi.org/10.1007/978-3-319-67925-9_1

74. Oussous, A., Benjelloun, F.-Z., Ait Lahcen, A., Belfkih, S.: Big data technologies: a survey. J. King Saud Univ. Comput. Inf. Sci. **30**(4), 431–448 (2018). https://doi.org/10.1016/j.jksuci.2017.06.001

75. Maheswari, N., Sivagami, M.: Large-scale data analytics tools: apache Hive, Pig, and HBase. In: Mahmood, Z. (ed.) Data Science and Big Data Computing: Frameworks and Methodologies, pp. 191–220. Springer, Cham (2016). https://doi.org/10.1007/978-3-319-318 61-5_9
76. Jaskaran Singh, V.S.: Big data tools and technologies in big data. Int. J. Comput. Appl. **112**(15) (2015)
77. Lydia, E.L., Swarup, D.M.B.: Big data analysis using Hadoop components like Flume, MapReduce, Pig and Hive. Int. J. Comput. Sci. Eng. Technol. **5**(11), 390–394 (2015)
78. Awad, A., Tommasini, R., Langhi, D., Kamel, M., Della Valle, E., Sakr, S.: D2IA: user-defined interval analytics on distributed streams. Inf. Syst. **104**, 101679 (2022). https://doi.org/10.1016/j.is.2020.101679
79. Arora, S., Agarwal, M.: Empowerment through big data: issues & challenges. Int. J. Sci. Res. Comput. Sci. Eng. Inf. Technol. **3**(5), 423–431 (2018). ISSN: 2456–3307, https://doi.org/10.32628/IJSRCSEIT
80. Nasiri, H., Nasehi, S., Goudarzi, M.: Evaluation of distributed stream processing frameworks for IoT applications in Smart Cities. J. Big Data **6**(1), 52 (2019). https://doi.org/10.1186/s40 537-019-0215-2
81. Talhaoui, M.A.: Real-time data stream processing - challenges and perspectives. Int. J. Comput. Sci. Issues **14** (2018). https://doi.org/10.20943/01201705.612
82. Saha, A.K., Kumar, A., Tyagi, V., Das, S.: Big data and internet of things: a survey. In: 2018 International Conference on Advances in Computing, Communication Control and Networking (ICACCCN), 12–13 Oct. 2018 2018, pp. 150–156 (2018). https://doi.org/10.1109/ICACCCN.2018.8748630
83. Hiraman, B.R., Chapte Viresh, M., Karve Abhijeet, C.: A study of apache kafka in big data stream processing. In: International Conference on Information, Communication, Engineering and Technology (ICICET), pp. 1–3 (2018). https://doi.org/10.1109/ICICET.2018.8533771
84. Gürcan, F., Berigel, M.: Real-time processing of big data streams: lifecycle, tools, tasks, and challenges. In: 2nd International Symposium on Multidisciplinary Studies and Innovative Technologies (ISMSIT), pp. 1–6 (2018). https://doi.org/10.1109/ISMSIT.2018.8567061
85. Wingerath, W., Gessert, F., Friedrich, S., Ritter, N.: Real-time stream processing for Big Data. IT Inf. Technol. **58**(4), 186–194 (2016). https://doi.org/10.1515/itit-2016-0002
86. Van-Dai, T., Chuan-Ming, L., Nkabinde, G.W.: Big data stream computing in healthcare real-time analytics. In: IEEE International Conference on Cloud Computing and Big Data Analysis (ICCCBDA), pp. 37–42 (2016). https://doi.org/10.1109/ICCCBDA.2016.7529531
87. Hagedorn, S., Götze, P., Saleh, O., Sattler, K.-U.: Stream processing platforms for analyzing big dynamic data. IT Inf. Technol. **58**(4), 195–205 (2016). https://doi.org/10.1515/itit-2016-0001
88. Salloum, S., Dautov, R., Chen, X., Peng, P.X., Huang, J.Z.: Big data analytics on Apache Spark. Int. J. Data Sci. Anal. **1**(3), 145–164 (2016). https://doi.org/10.1007/s41060-016-0027-9
89. Khalil, W.A., Torkey, H., Attiya, G.: Survey of Apache spark optimized job scheduling in big data. Int. J. Ind. Sustain. Dev. (IJISD) **1**(1), 39–48 (2020)

Towards Modeling Linguistic Fuzzy Basis Function Network Based on Hedge Algebra

Nguyen Van Han[1,2]($\boxtimes$) (iD)

[1] Faculty of Information Technology, Nguyen Tat Thanh University, 300A Nguyen Tat Thanh street, Ward 13, District 4, Ho Chi Minh City, Vietnam
nvhan@ntt.edu.vn
[2] Faculty of Electrical Engineering and Computer Science, VSB-Technical University of Ostrava, 17. listopadu 15, 708 33 Ostrava, Czech Republic

Abstract. This research presents a novel approach to modeling Linguistic Fuzzy Basis Function Networks (L-FBFNs) using Hedge Algebra (HA), which provides a robust framework for handling linguistic variables in fuzzy systems. Hedge Algebra offers a systematic method for quantifying linguistic terms, making it particularly suitable for applications requiring nuanced human-like reasoning. This study integrates HA with FBFNs to enhance their ability to process and interpret linguistic data. We propose a model that utilizes the inherent structure of HA to define fuzzy basis functions, thereby improving the interpretability and performance of the network in complex decision-making tasks.

The proposed L-FBFN model is validated through a series of benchmark tests, demonstrating its effectiveness in scenarios where traditional fuzzy systems may struggle. Results indicate that the incorporation of HA allows for more precise control over the fuzziness and granularity of linguistic terms, leading to superior performance in terms of both accuracy and computational efficiency. This work represents a significant advancement in the field of fuzzy logic and its applications, paving the way for more sophisticated and intuitive fuzzy systems in areas such as artificial intelligence, control systems, and data analysis. The findings underscore the potential of HA-based L-FBFNs to bridge the gap between computational models and human linguistic reasoning, fostering the development of more adaptive and intelligent systems.

Keywords: Linguistic Fuzzy Basis Function Network (L-FBFN) · Hedge Algebra (HA) · Fuzzy Systems · Fuzzy Basis Functions

1 Introduction

In the realm of fuzzy systems, the modeling of linguistic variables has long posed a challenge due to the inherent vagueness and imprecision of natural language. Traditional fuzzy systems [8,9], while effective in many applications, often struggle to capture the subtle nuances of human linguistic reasoning. This limitation

P. Cong Vinh et al. (Eds.): ICTCC 2024, LNICST 668, pp. 110–115, 2026.
https://doi.org/10.1007/978-3-032-12846-1_7

has spurred interest in more sophisticated methods for handling linguistic data, leading to the development of Linguistic Fuzzy Basis Function Networks (L-FBFNs).

Fuzzy Basis Function Networks (FBFNs) [5] are a powerful extension of conventional fuzzy systems, leveraging fuzzy basis functions to model complex relationships within linguistic data. These networks have demonstrated significant potential in various fields, including artificial intelligence, control systems, and data analysis. However, their effectiveness is often constrained by the methods used to quantify and interpret linguistic terms.

Hedge Algebra (HA) [3,4] offers a promising solution to this problem. HA provides a rigorous algebraic framework for the quantification of linguistic terms, facilitating more precise control over the fuzziness and granularity of linguistic variables. By integrating HA with L-FBFNs, it becomes possible to enhance the interpretability and performance of these networks, thereby improving their ability to process and analyze linguistic data.

The rest of the paper is organized as follows: Sect. 2 reviews related work on fuzzy neural networks and hedge algebra, highlighting the research gap that this paper addresses. Section 3 presents the theoretical framework, formally defining hedge algebra and its integration into LFNUs, describes the architecture of the proposed LFNU model, detailing each component and its role. Section 4 summaries outlines the corollary as well as future work.

2   Preliminary

This section summarizes the knowledge related to the article. These include hedge algebra (HA) and fuzzy neuron units (NUs).

2.1   Hedge Algebra

First definition of a HA is specified by 3-Tuple $\mathbb{HA} = (X, H, \leq)$ in [4]. In [3] to easily simulate fuzzy knowledge, two terms G and C are inserted to 3-Tuple so $\mathbb{HA} = (X, G, C, H, \leq)$ where $H \neq \emptyset$, $G = \{c^+, c^-\}$, $C = \{0, W, 1\}$. Domain of X is $\mathbb{L} = Dom(X) = \{\delta c \mid c \in G, \delta \in H^*(\text{hedge string over H})\}$, $\{\mathbb{L}, \leq\}$ is a POSET (partial order set) and $x = h_n h_{n-1} \ldots h_1 c$ is said to be a canonical string of linguistic variable x.

Example 1. Fuzzy subset X *is Age,* $G = \{c^+ = young;\ c^- = old\}$, $H = \{less; more; very\}$ *so term-set of linguistic variable Age X is* $\mathbb{L}(X)$ *or* $\mathbb{L}$ *for short:* $\mathbb{L} = \{very\ less\ young\ ;\ less\ young\ ;\ young\ ;\ more\ young\ ;\ very\ young\ ;\ very\ very\ young\ \ldots\}$

Fuzziness properties of elements in $\mathbb{HA}$, specified by *fm* (fuzziness measure) [3] as follows:

Definition 1. *A mapping fm* $: \mathbb{L} \to [0, 1]$ *is said to be the fuzziness measure of* $\mathbb{L}$*'s elements if:*

1. *fm is complate, i.e. $\sum_{c \in \{c^+, c^-\}} fm(c) = 1$, $fm(0) = fm(w) = fm(1) = 0$.*
2. *$\sum_{h_i \in H} fm(h_i x) = fm(x)$, $x = h_n h_{n-1} \dots h_1 c$, the canonical form.*
3. *for $\forall x, y \in \mathbb{L}$, for $\forall h \in H$*

$$\frac{fm(hx)}{fm(x)} = \frac{fm(hy)}{fm(y)}$$

This ratio does not depend on specific factors and is called fuzziness measure of hedge h , denoted by $\mu(h)$

Theorem 1. *in [4] let $\ell_1 = h_n \dots h_1 u$ and $\ell_2 = k_m \dots k_1 u$ be two arbitrary canonical representations of ℓ_1 and ℓ_2, then there exists an index $j \leq \bigwedge\{m, n\} + 1$ such that $h_i = k_j$, for $\forall i < j$, and:*

1. *$\ell_1 < \ell_2$ iff $h_j x_j < k_j x_j$ where $x_j = h_{j-1} \dots h_1 u$;*
2. *$\ell_1 = \ell_2$ iff $m = n = j$ and $h_j x_j = k_j x_j$;*
3. *ℓ_1 and ℓ_2 are incomparable iff $h_j x_j$ and $k_j x_j$ are incomparable;*

2.2   Fuzzy Basis Functions

Fuzzy Basis Functions (FBF) [5] are a powerful tool for combining the strengths of fuzzy logic and neural networks. They provide an interpretable, flexible, and robust way to model complex systems with uncertainty and imprecision, making them useful in various applications such as control systems, pattern recognition, and decision-making [6,8]. The FBF for node j in fuzzy basis function netwrok is defined as [5]

$$\phi_j(x) = \frac{\prod_{i=1}^{n} \mu_{A_i^j}(x_i)}{\sum_{j=1}^{M} (\prod_{i=1}^{n} \mu_{A_i^j}(x_i))} \tag{1}$$

The output equation of fuzzy system using centroid defuzzifier is expressed as:

$$y = \frac{\sum_{j=1}^{M} w_j (\prod_{i=1}^{n} \mu_{A_i^j}(x_i))}{\sum_{j=1}^{M} (\prod_{i=1}^{n} \mu_{A_i^j}(x_i))} \tag{2}$$

– Neural's inputs and weighs are numerical values in unit interval $[0, 1]$.

$$x_0 = 1$$

$$x = [x_0 \ x_1 \ x_2 \dots x_n]^T \in [0, 1]^{(n+1)}$$

$$w = [w_0 \ w_1 \ w_2 \dots w_n]^T \in [0, 1]^{(n+1)}$$

3   Modeling Linguistic Fuzzy Functions

The combinations of *Minimax* and *Maximin* have as many applications in decision making and optimization [7] as well as machine learning [1] and so on. Maximin applications of linguistic values have been applied in artificial intelligence as in [2]. This section is the first introduction to apply both *Maximin* and *Minimax* in neural units. This model allows direct computation on linguistic values. Reduces computational complexity because there is no need to perform intermediate operations in converting back and forth between numbers and linguistic values.

3.1   Definition and Architectural Model

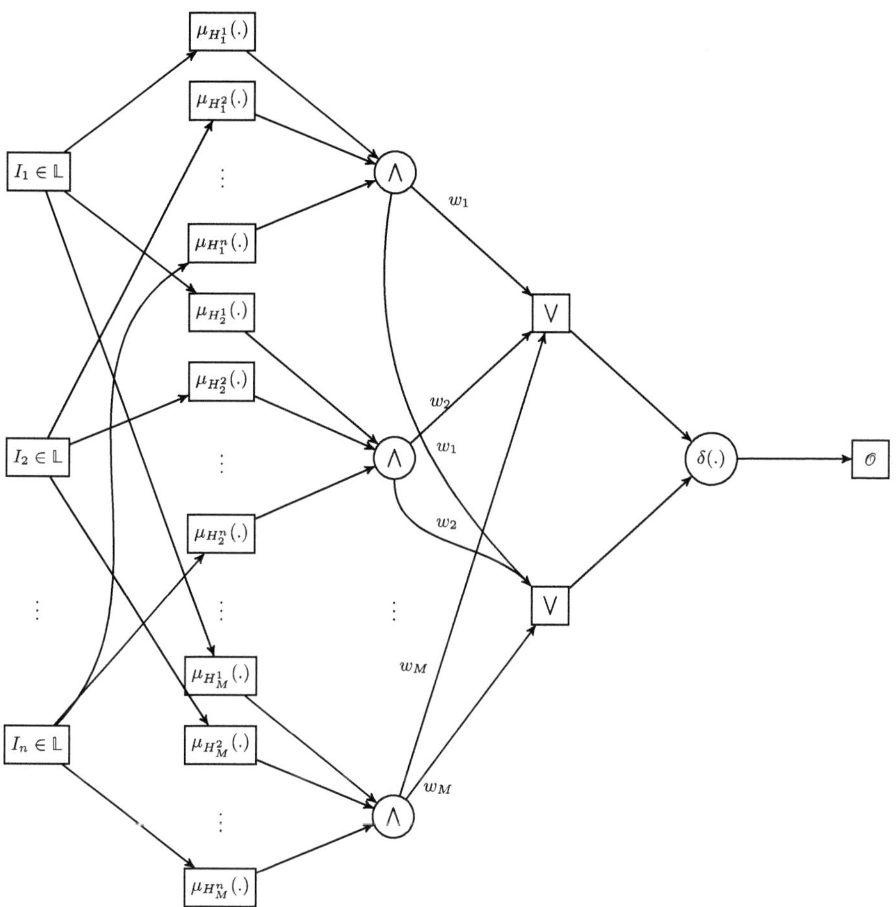

Fig. 1. A linguistic fuzzy basis function network

Definition 2. *A linguistic fuzzy basis function (LBF) consists of three sets*

- *Input set $\mathcal{I}$ and weigh $\mathcal{W}$:*

$$\mathcal{I} = [I_0\ I_1\ I_2 \ldots I_n]^T \in \mathbb{L}^{(n+1)}$$
$$\mathcal{W} = [w_0\ w_1\ w_2 \ldots w_n]^T \in \mathbb{L}^{(n+1)} \tag{3}$$

- *Linguistic fuzzy basis function*

$$\ell_j(I) = \frac{\bigwedge_{i=1}^{n} \mu_{H_i^j}(I_i)}{\bigvee_{j=1}^{M}\left(\bigwedge_{i=1}^{n} \mu_{H_i^j}(I_i)\right)} \tag{4}$$

- *Output set $\mathcal{O}$: The output equation of fuzzy system using centroid defuzzifier is expressed as:*

$$\mathcal{O} = \sum_{j=1}^{M} w_j \ell_j(I)$$

$$= \frac{\sum_{j=1}^{M} w_j (\bigwedge_{i=1}^{n} \mu_{H_i^j}(I_i))}{\bigvee_{j=1}^{M} (\bigwedge_{i=1}^{n} \mu_{H_i^j}(I_i))} \tag{5}$$

The Fig. 1 presents a linguistic basis function network, which consists of three layers

3.2 Algorithm and Applications

This section presents the pseudocode algorithm for input, output and computation of the LBF network. The pseudocode is presented as in Algorithm 1. Depending on the value of the delta function, LBF is applied in classification problems.

Algorithm 1. LBF network computational algorithm

Input: Input vectors $\mathcal{I} \in \mathbb{L}$ and wights $\mathcal{W} \in \mathbb{L}$
Output: Value $\mathcal{O}$
1: **for** $i \leftarrow 1$ to n **do**   ▷ Initialize values for *fuzzy concept*
2:     $I_i \in \mathbb{L}$
3: **end for**
4: **for** $j \leftarrow 1$ to M **do**   ▷ Computing for bocks $j = \overline{1, M}$
5:     $\ell_j(I) \leftarrow \dfrac{\bigwedge_{i=1}^{n} \mu_{H_i^j}(I_i)}{\bigvee_{j=1}^{M}(\bigwedge_{i=1}^{n} \mu_{H_i^j}(I_i))}$
6:     $\mathcal{O} \leftarrow \mathcal{O} + \ell_j(I)$
7: **end for**
8: **return** $\mathcal{O}$

---

4 Conclusion and Forthcoming Study

The article proposes a modeling with word based on fuzzy basis function.

- The linguistic fuzzy basis function and network.
- The algorithm to calulation of input and output with three layers of network.

In the future, two studies will be:

- Research on modeling and reasoning methods on deep structures of linguistic fuzzy basis function network.
- Research on applying for fuzzy basis function of linguistic models.

References

1. Ian, J., Goodfellow., Bengio, Y.: A hedge algebra linguistic cognitive map approach. ACM J. Reason. Words (2014)
2. Han, N.V., Vinh, P.C.: Reasoning with words: a hedge algebra linguistic cognitive map approach. Conc. Comput. Pract. Exper. **33**(2), e5711 (2020)
3. Ho, N.C., Son, T.T., Khang, T.D., Viet, L.X.: Fuzziness measure, quantified semantic mapping and interpolative method of approximate reasoning in medical expert systems. J. Comput. Sci. Cybern. **18**(3), 237–252 (2002)
4. Ho, N.C., Wechler, W.: Hedge algebras: an algebraic approach to structure of sets of linguistic truth values. Fuzzy Sets Syst. **35**(3), 281–293 (1990)
5. Guevara, J.M.M.J, Hirata, R.: Connections between fuzzy inference systems and kernel machines. In: IEEE International Conference on Fuzzy Systems (2020)
6. Gupta, L.J.M., Homma, N.: Static and Dynamic Neural Networks: From Fundamentals to Advanced Theory. First Edition, John Wiley & Sons (2003)
7. Gavalec, J.R.M., Zimmermann, K.: Decision Making and Optimization: Special Matrices and Their Applications in Economics and Management. Springer (2015)
8. Mendel, J.M.: Uncertain Rule-Based Fuzzy Systems: Introduction and New Directions. Springer (2017)
9. Mmdani, E.H.: Application of fuzzy logic to approximate reasoning using linguistic synthesis. IEEE Trans. Comput. **C-26**(12), 1182–1191 (1977)

Author Index

P. Cong Vinh et al. (Eds.): ICTCC 2024, LNICST 668, p. 117, 2026.
https://doi.org/10.1007/978-3-032-12846-1